THE TWO-IN-ONE
Walking with Smokie, Walking with Blindness

In the series
Animals, Culture, and Society,
edited by Clinton R. Sanders and Arnold Arluke

THE TWO-IN-ONE

Walking with Smokie,
Walking with Blindness

Rod Michalko

TEMPLE UNIVERSITY PRESS
Philadelphia

Temple University Press, Philadelphia 19122
Copyright © 1999 by Temple University Press
All rights reserved
Published 1999

Printed in the United States of America

∞ The paper used in this publication
meets the requirements of American National Standard for
Information Sciences—Permanence of Paper for Printed
Library Materials, ANSI Z39.48–1984

Library of Congress Cataloging-in-Publication Data
Michalko, Rod. 1946–
The two-in-one : walking with Smokie, walking with blindness / Rod Michalko.
    p.   cm. — (Animals, culture, and society)
Includes bibliographical references (p. 219) and index.
ISBN 1-56639-648-4 (alk. paper). — ISBN 1-56639-649-2 (pbk.: alk. paper)
1. Guide dogs.   2. Blindness—Psychological aspects.   3. Blind—Orientation
and mobility.   I. Title.   II. Series.
                            HV 1780.M53   1998
              362.4'183—dc21   98-20119
                                              CIP

For *Smokie*
For *Cassis, Jessie,* and *Sugar*
For *Bess* and *Jennie*

Contents

Acknowledgments

THE WRITING of this book was inspired by my experience with my dog guide, Smokie. Soon after meeting him in April, 1993, I realized that Smokie was giving me a great deal more than safe and efficient mobility. He gave me a different way to understand my blindness, a unique "look" at my world and he gave me a sense that blindness meant something more than the inability to see. This book is my attempt to capture the story of blindness as it came to me through the harness Smokie wears when he guides me.

I am especially indebted to Clint Sanders. He encouraged me to submit a manuscript for consideration for inclusion in a project on the human/non-human animal relationship which he was working on together with Temple University Press. Clint read drafts of chapters and provided me with insightful comments and suggestions throughout the writing of this book. Most importantly, Clint demonstrated an unequalled sensitivity to the particular relationship I have with Smokie and to the need to see the lessons inherent in this relationship.

I am also indebted to Janet Francendese, Editor-in-Chief of Temple University Press. Her comments on a draft of the first chapter I wrote were extremely helpful. I found our telephone conversations to be a special source of encouragement. Suzanne Wolk surpassed all my expectations of a copyeditor; she made me a much better writer and for this I am very grateful. I am indebted to Gord Taylor for patiently transcribing the mumblings from my dictaphone.

Spencer Cahill read my manuscript and provided a detailed and remarkably insightful evaluation. His comments were compelling and my book has taken on a richness because of them. I am extremely grateful for this.

My partner Dr. Tanya Titchkosky was an unending source of inspiration and encouragement throughout the writing of this book. As a sociologist, she read drafts with a critical eye and provided me with suggestions which are now woven throughout the pages of this book. Perhaps more than anyone else, Tanya knows what Smokie means to me. She also knows how important it was for me to write this book. We spent many hours discussing the value of writing a book that combines and integrates personal experience with sociological analysis. Most importantly, Tanya shared in the love that grew between Smokie and me and she continually taught me that this love releases the beginnings of a profound understanding of the mysterious relationship which exists between animals and people.

Most of all, I am indebted to Smokie. His paw prints are all over this book. I entered the dog guide school with the expectation of receiving a guide to mobility. But then I met Smokie. He is a guide to mobility, but he has given me much more than safety and efficiency of movement. Smokie has taught me that far from being a handicap, far from being an impairment or a disability, blindness is an occasion for me to make a place in the world and to be decisive about it. As Smokie and I work down a city street, I often forget about my blindness and focus on where he is guiding me and the world he is showing me. At the same time, Smokie compels me to experience my blindness and to treat this experience as an occasion to think about what is important. Smokie is my guide, my partner, and my friend. More than anything else, however, Smokie is my teacher. He guides in the true and ancient sense of that term; Smokie teaches as he guides. I will never be able to repay the debt I owe him. My gratitude to Smokie is as eternal as my love for him.

Chapter One
Introduction

I HAVE BEEN BLIND most of my life. The onset of my blindness occurred when I was a child. At that time, and for many years hence, my visual acuity was approximately 10 percent of what ophthalmologists refer to as "normal." Ten percent visual acuity falls within the legal definition of blindness and so, from the point of view of ophthalmology, I was blind. But from the point of view of my experience, I was not. After all, I could see—not much, but I could see. I could no longer play baseball, see the chalkboard from the back of the class-room, or recognize people from a distance—but I could see well enough to get around on my own.

As a child, I could not understand what was happening to my eyesight even when ophthalmologists or my parents explained it to me. I was confused and afraid. I did not know what was happening to me.

My eyesight stayed about the same until my late twenties, when I began to notice a gradual decrease in acuity. Even though I was no longer able to read print, I still had complete mobility without the use of a white cane or any other device. My life had not changed in any significant way.

The last five or six years, however, have been a different story. Unlike the gradual vision loss I experienced earlier, this most recent loss has been dramatic. It is as though I see things disappearing right before my eyes. As my partner Tanya puts it, "It seems as though you are going blind everyday. It is like you're going blind over and over again." Today I can distinguish light from dark, and what I do see, I see in the form of shadows.

Needless to say, my ability to "get around" has been severely hampered, and about five or six years ago I realized I would need help. I do not know why, but I did not want to use a white cane, so Tanya and I began to investigate the possibility of a dog guide. After researching several dog guide schools in both Canada and the United States, I chose a Canadian one. Two days after arriving at the school, I was introduced to my dog, Smokie. Smokie was fully trained and knew what he was doing. The same was not true of me. I spent a month at the school learning how to work Smokie. More importantly, Smokie and I spent this month getting to know one another, a process that continues to this day. Because the school was relatively close to our home, Tanya visited us a couple of times a week, and Smokie came to know her as well.

I was amazed at Smokie's abilities back then and I still am. He guides me everywhere safely and with a speed I have not known since my "10 percent days." Smokie knows how to find everything I need—doors, chairs, escalators, telephones, stairs. He guides me down busy city streets and I rarely even rub shoulders with another pedestrian. I do not take Smokie's abilities for granted, even after five years. Smokie's seemingly effortless ability to distinguish left from right still makes me smile with admiration. Getting me safely where I want to go is what Smokie has done for me, and this is important. But even more important, Smokie has re-introduced me to my blindness.

I had certainly been introduced to it before. Losing most of my eyesight when I was a child, and most all the rest of it in adulthood, was quite an introduction. Ordinary life was no longer ordinary; everything was wrapped in a cloak of anxiety. Before losing the rest of my sight, I used to do things the way everyone else did; I just did them. I just walked around, just played sports, just read, just met people at cafés, just looked and just saw. I didn't have to think about it.

Then *blindness,* and with it, anxiety, fear, and confusion. I could no longer "just" do things; I had to think about every step and every move. Blindness took the "just" out of "just doing things." Some tasks I could no longer perform at all, while others required a complete re-education. I saw everything differently now and I had to think about everything in a whole new way.

There were those who helped me find new ways to do old things. This "help," however, came with a certain conception of blindness. Most people, including ophthalmologists and other professionals, think of blindness as a physiological phenomenon that has a negative effect on peoples' lives. Our society conceives of blindness in terms of "lack"—lack of sight. But this conception does not really help us understand what blindness *itself* is. It does not generate any curiosity about what blind people "see," since it defines reality in terms of the physical sense of sight. Whatever blind persons see is, by definition, a distortion of reality. They must therefore learn to "adjust" to reality as it is understood by the dominant culture. Sighted people seldom question these preconceptions. They take blindness at face value and assume that there is nothing more to be said about it or learned from it.

This attitude was one of the first things I confronted when I became blind, and I have spent the past decade examining it. My training in sociology helped me begin to understand that the common view of blindness is, in fact, a cultural construct and, as such, that it has limitations that perhaps can be transcended. I began to see both blindness and sightedness as "cultures" possessing different customs, norms, and belief systems. It was a small step from there to understand blindness in terms of the sociological dichotomy of deviance and conformity. Blindness is a culturally constructed concept even when spoken of as a physiological fact. I worked with this concept for many years.

Smokie, however, introduced me to still another way of looking at blindness. When he became a part of my life, I was encouraged to re-think both the prevailing view of blindness as a negative physiological phenomenon and my own conception of blindness as a form of "cultural deviance." I had thought that my own formulation was an advance, and that I needed only to continue my research along those lines. Smokie's presence in my life taught me otherwise. His approach to blindness is of a different nature altogether.

This book is my attempt to articulate that approach

and to describe what I have learned from Smokie about blindness and a great many other things. Through telling the story of Smokie and me, I will attempt to tell the story of blindness as it unfolds through the paradigms of personhood, nature, and society. This story is told through an "interpretive chain": it is about a relationship between a blind person and a dog guide, which is in the first place a relationship between a person and a dog but also a relationship between society and nature. This book is about *that* relationship.

The links in this interpretive chain are ontologically interdependent; they rely upon one another not only for their sense and meaning but for their very being. As an animal, Smokie symbolically represents nature while I, as a person, do the same in relation to society. The bond between Smokie and me may be understood as the bond between nature and society. Smokie and I do not merely inhabit a common natural and social world; we depend upon one another for our existence, and together we construct and re-construct the world. Smokie and I are, almost literally, extensions of each other, and the interpretive chain that we inhabit takes the form of a circle (Gadamer 1986) rather than a straight line.

This book explores the relation between nature and society that is presupposed in the partnership between a blind person and dog guide. It examines the choices we humans make in our relation to nature and attempts to draw out the practical implications of those choices. The partnership between me and Smokie is embedded in a much wider realm of activity and interaction. Through the lens of our relationship, I will explore the decision to use dogs for guiding work, the training of dogs as guides, cultural conceptions of blindness and of dog guides, and the social world through which blind persons and their dogs move and live.

I begin in chapter two, "Search for a Guide," by examining the often implicit connection between the concept of "guiding" and the dog. Most of us conceive of blindness as an obstacle to full participation in social life that must be overcome or adjusted to. Blind people can come to know the world through senses other than sight and can participate in this world through a variety of techniques and technologies. Success at this depends upon the degree of vision loss, age of onset, historical time and place, and other social, psychological, and political factors.

All blind persons do, however, require some form of guidance. Its extent will vary from the simplest to the most complex, from asking the location of a telephone to learning subtle visual concepts such as where walls meet ceilings. The amount and kind of guidance needed will also depend on whether a person was born blind or lost vision gradually. Whatever the individual circumstances, guidance is an essential part of blind people's lives.

It is difficult to move through the world without seeing, or seeing very little. Most people take walking down the street for granted. Blind persons do not. We rely on our remaining senses to guide us. Some of us also rely on white canes; others rely on dog guides. All of us, from time to time, rely on sighted people for guidance. Guiding not only allows mobility but also implicitly imparts a conception of the world. The connection between blindness and guiding assumes the sense of touch as the "distance sense," and I will show how the senses are re-organized to allow touch its new status and how the sense of touch is enhanced by the choice of an appropriate guide. This chapter will also discuss how guiding has come to be connected with dogs and will explore the assumptions and presuppositions that make it possible to think about dogs as guides for blind persons in the first place.

A blind person leaves a dog guide training school with more than a dog. She leaves with the school's conception of blindness, its conception of the dog, and its understanding of how the person and dog should relate. The blind person also leaves with her own interpretation of those conceptions, and the interpretive process continues throughout her life with the dog. Chapter three, "Is That One of Those Blind Dogs?", examines the particular concept of blindness held by those who train dog guides and deals with the training, application, and screening processes used by dog guide schools.

Dog guides are trained with an "ideal type" (Weber 1947, 89–110) of blind person in mind; but most blind persons do not use dog guides, and not every blind person is accepted for training with a dog guide. All dog guide training provides an implicit answer to the question, "What kind of guiding does a blind person need?" By making use of my own experience at a dog guide training school as well as the experience of others, I will show the ways in which these schools answer this question. In the process, I hope to show how the person and the dog together constitute the various meanings and conceptions of blindness, and to explore the ways in which the dog guide "releases" blindness into the social world as the dog guide team moves through it. This will involve a discussion of Smokie as a particular dog, as well as a more general discussion of the dog's relation to human society.

Chapter four, "The Grace of Teaching," examines the dog guide's influence on the blind person's experience and conception of blindness. Dog guides are not merely functional; they are neither robots nor pieces of equipment like white canes. They are *guides* in the fullest sense of the word; they not only help take a person from place to place but also help direct her conduct or course of life. In their guiding, they are also constantly *teaching* the blind person—both about the physical and social environment and also about what it means to be blind. More often than not, a dog guide changes a blind person's experience of blindness in fundamental ways.

A dog guide not only enables a blind person to be more mobile and independent but also—when the two are fully "in tune" with each other—to move through the world with a "graceful independence." This independence is achieved through the "togetherness" of dog and blind person, yet both also experience an "aloneness." I address this experience of a dog-guide team through a concept that I call the "alone-together."

Perhaps one of the most interesting things about having a dog guide is that it brings blindness to the fore in public places. Smokie and I are not anonymous travellers in our world. Everyone notices us. And when they do, they see certain things about us. When people notice Smokie and me they see us through their particular conceptions of blindness, of dog guides, and of the partnership between the two. Usually, however, people do more than notice us; more often than not, they talk to us, and that provides an education in itself. I have learned a great deal about people's conceptions of blindness from their comments on the street, and one of the things I have learned is the degree to which Smokie and I are preceded by our "reputation." People have concepts about us before they see us; in a way, that is what enables them to notice us in the first place. People are always talking either to or about us—quite often, both. Chapter five, "The Power of Reputation," and chapter six, "Feel Free to Ask," describe some of this interaction and analyze the relationship between our identity and how we are perceived by others.

Whatever Smokie and I do, whatever kind of life we experience together and whatever else we mean to each other, we are "person and dog" sharing a life together. We are "human and animal" living in the world and moving through it together. I rely on Smokie for my safety, for my independence, and for whatever semblance of grace I may possess. Smokie depends on me for the provision of his basic needs—food, water, shelter, and love. He also relies on me for his identity as a dog guide, as a working animal. Smokie's presence in his harness depicts my blindness to the world and my presence depicts his working identity. Our interdependence shows the world around us who we are and what we mean together; it allows, in Goffman's (1959) terms, the presentation of *our self* in everyday life. This is the nature of our bond.

More than this, Smokie and I represent the bond and relation that exists between human life and natural life. My life with Smokie has given me the opportunity to re-think this relation. Smokie's presence in my life has reminded me that "nature" is as much a cultural construction as "blindness" is, and that distinctions like human/ animal, society/nature, nature/nurture are themselves human inventions. By explicating the assumptions and presuppositions that underlie the distinction between the social and natural worlds, I will show that such distinctions, together with the relationships that follow from them, are the result of implicit interpretive choices.

The concluding chapter, "The Two-In-One," is a reflection on what my life with Smokie has taught me about the nature/nurture distinction as it exists within me, the individual. Blindness itself expresses this distinction. Blindness is physiological insofar as it expresses itself within the paradigm of the "natural function" of seeing. Yet we, as individuals in society, *make* something of blindness. We endow blindness with meaning through the ways we think about and interpret it. The shifting and ever-changing character of human concerns, purposes, and interests makes blindness something which itself exhibits a variety of meanings. The same is true of nature and of the connection between nature and society. The aim of this chapter is to interrogate the society/nature distinction.

Shortly after I had completed this book, we moved from Toronto to Antigonish, Nova Scotia. Toronto has a population of over two million, while Antigonish numbers approximately 5,000. This is an incredible difference! I have addressed in an epilogue some of the significant implications of this difference for Smokie and me.

This book is my attempt to capture and depict the experience of moving through the world with a dog guide, and to examine my reasons for writing it in the first place. My need to think about blindness and about my relation to nature and society has led me to explore the collective representations of nature with which this society makes sense of itself. The result is a narrative account of what I have learned about myself and my world with Smokie as my guide. We invite and welcome readers to "our world."

Chapter Two
Search for a Guide

"[A dog guide is] really like a car for sighted people. You drive it for a number of years and then get a new one. It's just like that."
— Staff member at a dog guide school

I LISTENED INTENTLY as I stood at the top of the stairway leading down to the subway platform. My right hand clung tightly to the metal banister as I felt for the first step with my left foot. The lighting of the subway station contrasted dramatically with the bright sunshine outside. It was dark. I could see only shadows.

I heard movement on the stairs. A rush of people ascended and I waited for the shadows and sound to disappear. In a few seconds it would be safe. I tentatively took the first step and proceeded down the stairs slowly, feet and right hand my only guides.

Suddenly I touched something with my left knee. It was a gentle touch, but a touch nonetheless. Just as suddenly, the voice of a woman: "No, out of his way. Come over here." The touch I felt was a child! The anxiety that rushed through my body froze me. I had almost knocked a child down two flights of stairs. There was no question now. I needed help.

Somehow I managed to get home. Still shaken, I told my partner Tanya what had happened. For some time now, she had been encouraging me to seek help in getting around. Every time I left our house, she would express concern for my safety. On this afternoon, I finally agreed. I needed help.

Since I did not want to use the white cane, Tanya began insisting that I acquire a dog guide. I had had dogs as pets before and she knew that I liked them. Tanya also liked dogs and suggested that a dog guide would not only help me get around but would be a great addition to our family, which at that time included Tanya and me and two cats, Jessie and Sugar. Reminding me of my "days as an athlete," Tanya suggested that a dog would be a much more appropriate guide than a white cane. A dog would be energetic and quick, like an athlete; a dog would be good for me. She began researching dog guide schools and brought home several books on dogs and their training from the library.

A few days after my experience on the subway, Tanya telephoned from the library and we arranged to meet at a downtown bar to discuss her research. As was my habit, I arrived at the bar early. Whenever I met someone I arrived early so that they would have to look for me and not the other way around. I made my way into the bar and down a short flight of stairs, found a table, and, hoping no one else was sitting there, sat down.

The waiter asked if I would like something to drink and I ordered a pint of draft beer. He said that he would serve me only coffee. I was confused, to say the least. Naively, I asked him if there was something wrong with the mechanism on the beer kegs. No, the kegs worked fine. The look on my face must have betrayed my confusion. "I think you've had enough to drink," he said. My confusion turned to extreme embarrassment. I explained that I was "legally blind" and showed the waiter my identification card. His apologies only added to my embarrassment. He insisted that I have a beer and I insisted on coffee.

A few minutes later, Tanya joined me and I told her what had happened. We both recognized the comic character of the incident, but we also saw its tragic side. This sort of thing had never happened to me before, but it was yet another sign of the things I could no longer see. Things were changing quickly, and as she had many times before, Tanya said, "It's like you are going blind over and over again." Even though I felt uncomfortable, Tanya and I spent the rest of the afternoon in the bar discussing dog guides.

Our conversation led us in a direction we had not taken before. "Getting around" had always been the focus of previous conversations. Getting around without a guide was confusing not only to me but to others. Things were disappearing quickly and what I saw at one time, I could not see at another. Shadows confused me; I often saw them as objects and moved quickly to avoid them. Things I could see in twilight disappeared in bright sunshine. Children stood on empty stairways. I was "drunk," only to be blind a few moments later.

But now the need to "get around" led Tanya and me to recognize my need to "*be* around." "Getting around" was transformed from an abstraction into *my* very particular movement through *my* particular world. However I did it, I would have to get around as *me*, as *who I am*.

That afternoon in the bar, Tanya and I realized that our discussions about dog guides were discussions about *identity*—mine, hers, and ours together.

Who I was was someone going blind "over and over again." It seemed as though I was continually going blind but never quite getting there. I could not count on my little bit of sight, but I could not discount it, either. It was there in the morning and gone in the afternoon, only to return in the evening. Things appeared and disappeared right before my eyes. "Being around" in this way was as difficult as "getting around."

The dog guide, we thought, would go a long way toward solving these problems. A dog would get me around safely. Everyone would see the harness and know that I was blind, not drunk. My journey to blindness would be over—I would finally get there. I had no idea that the acquisition of a dog guide would mark the beginning of a never-ending journey with blindness, and I did not realize how many "blindnesses" the dog would guide me to.

As we spoke in the bar that afternoon, Tanya and I grew more and more excited about the prospect of a dog guide. Tanya even raised the possibility of "enjoying" blindness. Though I was skeptical, I did understand that a dog guide would somehow place blindness squarely in our life. Sight had always accompanied me as I moved through the world. I would now be leaving sight behind and accepting blindness as my partner. I would still have my "little bit of sight"; I could still see shadows. But sight would no longer be an essential, defining feature of *my identity*. A dog guide would *make* me blind.

The relationship I had always assumed between blindness and sightedness was quickly losing its cogency. I no longer thought of them as strict opposites, or even, necessarily, as antithetical. I was not sure what their relationship was; it was more complicated than I'd thought, but its exact nature eluded me.

The connection between blindness and sightedness is located somewhere in the murkiness of our social identities. It lurks in the nexus of our natural and social being and in the relationship between nature and society. It is natural to see and unnatural not to. But what do these terms mean?

I wanted to take a closer look at the connection between seeing and not seeing, between what is natural and what is not. I began with the work of David Michael Levin.

THE GIFT OF VISION

Vision is nature's gift of a possible *adventure* in the social, or cultural order. . . . What we do with our natural endowment—how we respond to the gift of nature—constitutes the *character* of our vision. Whether, and how, we take up our visionary project: that is the measure, the test, of our character, of our development of self. . . . For the most part, our vision conforms, conforms to the gaze of a social order which reflects and multiplies our fears, ignorance and passions, and which extinguishes many of the sparks that might otherwise kindle some effort of vision. . . . The loss occurs because curiosity is the arousing of desire, and it is desire which brings about the more restricted form of vision, which is more interested in the objects brought forth by the

lighting of the field than it is open to the enchantment in the presence of the lighting itself. (Levin 1988,
56, 59)

Levin's work implies a distinction between sight and
vision which suggests that sight *alone* does not really *see*.
Sight is nature and *only* nature. As such, it sees nothing,
not even itself. It is the social order that enables sight to
"see"; sight is socially organized. Sight represents the
possibility of vision but is itself not vision. Vision is a natural endowment, a gift from nature which requires development. How we look and what we see is our response to
that gift. Every life is a "gifted life" insofar as it is naturally endowed with the gift of vision. It is also a "gift of
possible adventure." Adventure becomes possible in the
mixing of the natural and social orders. What we make of
our natural endowments in the context of social life is a
measure and test of our self-development.

Nature gives us vision at the moment of our immersion
into a social and cultural order. We see in and through
this order on each and every occasion of our looking.
Nature enters the realm of the social whenever it gives
the gift of vision, whenever we look. When we look, nature *offers* us the gift of a possible adventure. The *character*
of our vision is determined by our response to this gift.
The gift of nature is expressed in the dialogue between
nature and society and our possibility of adventure lies in
whether, and how, we enter this dialogue as interlocutors. This is what Levin calls the "visionary project."

But Levin also warns us of vision's tendency to conform.
It conforms to the "gaze" of the social order. Conformity
always presupposes complicity. When it conforms, vision
complies with the gaze of social order; vision looks at

what social order provides for it to see. It then reflects and multiplies our "fears, ignorance and passions," and thus sustains and reproduces the social order as the "paramount reality" (Schutz 1973, 226f).

Conformity to the social order "extinguishes many of the sparks that might otherwise kindle some effort of vision." Looking and seeing only in socially and culturally prescribed ways is to reject nature's gift. It is to reflect the gaze of social order and that gaze only. Levin suggests that when vision conforms, as it usually does, it sees only "the objects brought forth by the lighting of the field" but misses "the enchantment in the presence of the lighting itself." Conformity restricts our "field of vision" and requires no effort on our part. We see what is there to see and nothing else. We see only what is already lighted. What is "natural" about vision, in this sense, is that it reveals the social and cultural order as the "natural" order of things.

VISION LOSS

Vision conceived in this way has consequences for those of us who are blind. To be blind is to be born without the natural endowment of vision or to lose it at some point in one's life. Those who are congenitally blind were never given the gift of vision; adventitiously blind persons were given the gift only to have it revoked, usually by nature.

Vision that conforms to the social order takes the reality of what is seen as fixed and final. It approaches the possibility of vision loss with fear and anticipates the result of that loss as ignorance. Vision loss is understood as the physiological loss of sight, of the ability to

'ects brought forth by the lighting of the
we cannot see those objects, we stumble
—we do not know them; we are ignorant.

⌐ındness, conventionally understood, means the fear of stumbling through the world in ignorance. How, then, could it possibly be conceived as a gift of nature? To see is to live in full knowledge of the world; not to see is to live in ignorance. To see is to be guided through the sights and objects of the world; not to see is to stumble. To see is to be guided into full participation in the world; not to see is to be denied access. It is no wonder that vision is considered a gift. It *is* a gift; it is the quintessential "guide" that opens the world to us and presents us with "possible adventures," our response to which tests and measures our character.

Blindness means facing the world without benefit of a guide. Without it, the possibilities of movement, knowledge and participation are threatened. The fundamental problem of blindness thus becomes the search for a guide. Blind persons must find a way into the horizon of possibilities ordinarily and "naturally" provided by the gift of vision. Whether and how blind persons take up this quest is the measure and test of their character and self-development. Embarking on this quest is the blind person's "visionary project."

Like sighted people, blind people must pursue this project in the context of their society and culture. "Actual blind persons"[1] find themselves always-already immersed in socially organized meanings that depict *what* blindness is and *who* blind people are; Durkheim (1915) called these social meanings "collective representations." The quest for a guide takes place within these "collective representations" and, following Levin, it is certainly an adventure.

THE NECESSITY OF GUIDANCE

After my experience in the subway and after being mistaken for drunk in the bar, I finally agreed with Tanya. I could no longer continue with blindness alone. I needed a guide not only to get around, but also to "guide" others to the understanding that I was blind. This realization came somewhat more slowly to my friends than to Tanya. Since I did not use a white cane or dog guide, many people were not aware that I was blind. I never disclosed my blindness to people upon our initial meeting. If our relationship continued or the situation warranted it— for example, if I was looking for a book in a bookstore— that was different. My friends and coworkers certainly knew that I was blind but most others did not.

My blindness usually remained unspoken, even in my interactions with friends. But the more sight I lost, the louder my blindness spoke.[2] I met friends in neighborhood bars and cafés and told them about the difficulty I had getting there. Many of them adopted a strictly pragmatic approach. One evening, for example, having a beer with two friends at a neighborhood bar, I went to the men's room. When I returned, I said, "Jeez, I couldn't see a thing." My friend Gord replied, "Well, just get one of those white sticks."

The more my friends and I spoke about my blindness, however, the more confusing our interaction became. For a long time I had had little difficulty getting around, but this had changed rapidly. Previously I had been defined, both by myself and by others, as someone who could see, even if not very much. Now, however, I could see even less than that. Friends often forgot this. I would ask where something was and someone would point. I would say, "What! Are you pointing?" The friend would reply, "Right, I forgot. Next time tell me." People would often say, "I forgot you were blind. You have to remind me."

I often did the same thing. I "forgot" I was blind and acted like someone who could see. This forgetting was the result not so much of a faulty memory as of a confused and confusing identity. My identity was in the process of being transformed; I was in a "grey area" both literally and figuratively. Part of this confusion stemmed from the absence of a visible sign of my blindness. Since I did not use a guide, there was no outward indication to serve as a reminder to others. I usually met friends in familiar places where I knew my way around fairly well. Even so, my blindness and my need for a guide were becoming more apparent.

The form a guide will take depends on how blindness is conceived. The first response to blindness is always curative. Can the blind person's sight be restored? If not, what can substitute for sight? How can she move through the world now that she is missing sight? The form of a blind person's social adventure depends on how these questions are answered. How we answer them shapes our conceptions of blindness and our relations to it; it defines our social relations with blindness. How we conceive of and relate to blindness reveals, as Karatheodoris (1982) says, an answer to the question, "What is blindness?" All interaction with blindness simultaneously poses and answers this question.

A blind person's search for a guide, then, is always conducted in a social order that understands eyesight as the "natural guide"; as such it becomes a search for something that will replace nature with something "person-created." This *made-in-society* guide is always "second-best" to the natural one, always "unnatural" in relation to the natural gift of vision. Made in society, made by people, it is *techne*.

THE SEARCH FOR A GUIDE AS A VISIONARY PROJECT

My "visionary project" was an intense and difficult quest. It was not a purely practical matter, because I did not see this project as finding a straightforward solution to a straightforward problem. A blind lawyer told me that "all it [blindness] is, is a nuisance and an inconvenience." I had experienced plenty of nuisances and inconveniences in my life, but my blindness did not feel like any of them. I could not get rid of it by implementing various practical solutions. To the contrary, I experienced blindness as a problem that would be with me for the rest of my life.

I had been "getting around" for many years with eyesight whose acuity fell within the bounds of legal blindness, often "passing"[3] as sighted. I acted and interacted as if I could see, and in some sense, I could. But even this "sense" eventually left me.

Even so, I still moved through the world using a multitude of interactional cues. They were the same cues I had employed when I could still see a little. I walked down sidewalks listening intently for any sign of pedestrian traffic—footsteps, talking, coughing, laughter. I travelled only in familiar areas unless I was with someone who could see. Rather than risk accidentally sitting on someone, I stood on public transportation, pretending to prefer standing to sitting. I received many of my cues through listening and smelling and many more through my common-sense knowledge of social settings. I could easily locate ashtrays in cafés and bars since they were usually to be found nestled among the salt and pepper shakers on the table. As a precaution, however, I skimmed my hand along the tabletop in case the ashtray were somewhere else. Friends also helped me "pass," even though that was not their intention. When I walked with a friend, I would make sure that I was half a step behind while still walking side by side. In this way, I was both following and being guided. Tanya and I always held hands when we walked, another way of guiding.

Eventually, though, moving through the world became more and more difficult. I required more time to react to obstacles on the sidewalk, including pedestrians, and I slowed my walking pace. Whenever I heard, smelled, or felt something disorienting or unfamiliar, I stopped walking altogether. I stood still, attending to my environment intently, until I was once again oriented. My remaining senses and common-sense knowledge of the social world acted as my guide, and they served me well. But the continual need to halt and reorient myself made me realize that I needed a new guide, or at least a supplement to my old ones.

I first considered a white cane. This did not reflect a decision that a cane would be appropriate for me, but a resolve to do what was inevitable. I needed help "getting around" and the white cane automatically came to mind, and with it, all that it symbolized. It brought my blindness to mind, especially the limits it put on me. I knew that a white cane would not restore my ease and confidence. It would only make walking safer; it would enable me to detect obstacles and show others that I was blind. This recognition by others would only reinforce the inevitable character of my blindness. Considering the cane as a guide to mobility made me aware of the *pathos* of blindness. The cane was an unmistakable sign of labored and graceless movement. Its whiteness suggested naïve vulnerability. The white cane represented sheer necessity without choice.

Negative and biased as it was, this was my sense of the white cane. I had learned how to use the cane years earlier as part of my research on rehabilitation practices for blind persons. Now I began using it again, but I was not as resolute about the decision to use it as I was about the inevitable "fact" of my blindness. I found that my speed and confidence did not increase significantly, and the ever-present *pathos* filled me with an unease that I could not readily identify. Becoming a skilled user of the white cane was not particularly challenging, and I felt no sense of mastery. I did not experience the cane as an extension of my body or as a part of myself. I soon discarded it and reverted to my original mode of travel, which was not as safe but was at least free of *pathos.*

With determined encouragement from Tanya, I began to consider a dog guide. Although I liked dogs, I was not comfortable with the idea of being guided by one. I found it difficult to trust the idea that someone other than myself could act as a full-time guide. In my experience as a blind person and in my research on blindness, I had met several dog guide teams. For the most part, they had impressed me as ineffective. I had seen many blind persons become lost and disoriented while using their dog guides. Many dog guides I saw moved extremely slowly and tentatively on city streets. I also felt sympathy for the dogs while they worked in the midst of car pollution and extreme heat or cold. Many of the dog guides I saw were overweight and looked unhealthy. I was wary of the dog as an effective guide.

Nonetheless, I put my reservations aside while Tanya and I reviewed the literature on dog guides. We discovered that not much had been written on the topic. The social sciences, for example, were only beginning to address the phenomenon of "working dogs" and only recently had they begun to show any interest in animal/ human relations.[4] The works that existed included personal accounts of assistant dog use and a few historical accounts.

We began gathering information from various schools that train dog guides. Other than the details of application procedures, we did not learn very much; there was next to nothing about the schools' philosophies or training processes. Finally we visited a Canadian school close to our home, and this was the school I eventually attended.

When we arrived, one of the administrative staff took us for a tour of the facilities. Among the many questions I raised with our tour guide, I asked how long a dog guide was typically expected to work. This was her response:

> On the average, they work until they're about ten years old. But this varies from dog to dog. The good thing is that you retire them and then get a new one. It's really like a car for sighted people. You drive it for a number of years and then get a new one. It's just like that.

Depicted in this very mechanical way, dog guides are mobility "devices" in a literal sense. The car analogy could be invoked only with respect to mobility; beyond that the comparison of cars and dog guides obviously falls apart. We were deeply disappointed that such a conception even existed at the school.

Shortly after this exchange, the staff member introduced us to a trainer. He had a dog guide with him, a yellow Labrador Retriever named Leo. The trainer removed Leo's harness and allowed us to meet him. After Leo's enthusiastic greeting, we spoke with the trainer about the school's training methods. He told us that the dogs were trained strictly on a program of rewards. No corrections were given to the dog until it "understood" what the trainer expected it to do.

This was a gratifying corrective to the mechanistic analogy. The trainer asked if I wanted to "see" what the harness felt like on Leo. He took Leo's leash, held the harness in front of him and gave the command "harness." Leo stepped into his harness and the trainer fastened it. He then heeled Leo around to my left side and showed me how to hold the leash between my index and middle fingers and how to grasp the harness handle in my left hand. I felt a slight tension emanating from the harness as Leo stood there, leaning forward but not moving. My left arm was extended down and out and most of Leo's body was in front of me. I experienced a sudden and surprising sense of security. I was holding the harness handle lightly in my hand as the trainer instructed me to do, but in spite of the lightness of my grasp, I felt a sense of stability that seemed to come from the firmness and strength of Leo's shoulders. I also experienced a sense of *distance,* an *expansion* of my immediate environment. It seemed as though my "sense of touch" was enhanced by Leo and his harness. I could "feel" further than I ever had before. Harness and Leo in hand, I felt my tactile sense replacing my sense of sight as the "distance sense."[5]

The trainer interrupted this absorbing sensation by saying that I could give Leo the command "forward." "Just tell him forward, take a few steps, and then tell him to stay." He told me to say the dog's name to get his attention before commanding him "forward," and to do the same when commanding him to "stay."

With an exaggerated sense of expectancy, I flexed my fingers around the harness and said "Leo, forward." The movement was exhilarating. Leo moved us forward with a strength and confidence I had not experienced since my "10 percent days." He was almost a body length in front of me.[6] It was as though I could "see" several feet ahead. The harness tightened as Leo pulled and I followed. After more than a few steps, I remembered to ask Leo to "stay." The trainer instructed me to praise him. I dropped the harness handle, knelt beside Leo, patted him and told him he was a good boy. He returned my praise with several licks. My "search for a guide" was over. I knew my guiding needs would by fulfilled by a dog.

A dog was appealing to me for several reasons. Unlike the white cane, a dog is a living being with needs, wants, and emotional responses. Working a dog guide requires the development of an emotional bond, whereas the white cane simply evokes emotions, in my case, negative ones. The inanimate white cane *could* be named but a dog *must* have a name if the dog is expected to respond.[7]

Once I had experienced the sensation of holding Leo

in his harness, my decision was made. The essential factor was how the dog guide animated and expanded my "field of touch." Leo seemed to bring my physical environment closer to me. Six points of physical contact were transmitted to me through the harness handle—my two feet and Leo's four. I experienced these six points tactilely in the form of security, stability, strength, and a sense of distance. In those first few steps with Leo, my sense of touch seemed to focus my attention on the expanded horizon of my physical environment. I was truly being guided.

THE DISTANCE SENSE

The idea of the tactile sense becoming the distance sense was expressed clearly to me in an interview I conducted with a three-year-old boy, Mark, who was born totally blind. We were sitting on the floor of his living room, rolling a ball back and forth. At one point, the ball hit Mark's foot and bounced away. He began "looking" for it, searching with his hands, stretching his arms out as far as he could. After a short while, Mark gave up his search. He said that his "Mommy could find it." "Can she?" I asked. "Yeah," he replied, "cause she can see." I asked him how he knew this and he answered, "Cause she's got really, really, really long arms."

The "cuteness" and the *pathos*[8] of Mark's response notwithstanding, it clearly depicts tacticity as the distance sense. Hearing and smell also play a role in experiencing distant objects, but it is the sense of touch that brings those objects into the immediate experience of contact. Mark may have heard the ball bounce off his foot and he certainly felt it. Hearing did play a role in

Mark's experience of the ball as "somewhere in the distance." But contact with the ball, for Mark, depended on the sense of touch. Eyesight was irrelevant to him. What he needed for contact with the ball was not eyesight but longer arms.

Diderot (1982, 77–78) speaks of this need in his "Letter on the Blind for the Use of Those Who See."

> One of our company bethought him of asking our blind man if he would like to have eyes. "If it were not for curiosity," he replied, "I would just as soon have long arms: It seems to me my hands would tell me more of what goes on in the moon than your eyes or your telescopes; and besides, eyes cease to see sooner than hands to touch. I would be as well off if I perfected the organ I possess, as if I obtained the organ which I am deprived of."

Eyesight is a curious thing for persons who are blind, especially for the congenitally blind. Not surprisingly, blind persons are more curious about eyesight than those who take eyesight for granted. For the most part, curiosity about eyesight is restricted to those who experience the "mystery of the eye" through the "shadow of blindness."

Were it not for his curiosity, Diderot's blind man would rather have long arms than eyes. This blind man contemplates what he would be given were he given eyes. Eyes would give him the ability to experience distant objects like the moon. The gift of eyesight would endow him with the possibility of adventure that springs from an expanded visual universe. The blind man's world, spatially framed by his body (his reach), his hearing, and his sense of smell would be expanded if he had sight. With sight, and its enhancement by telescopes, he could sensually experience an object as distant as the moon. The blind man knows that eyes would enable him to experience distance in a whole new way, yet he rejects this possibility, in spite of his curiosity.

Why? Because, he says, his hands would tell him more about the moon than his eyes could. What can eyes tell him about the moon other than that it is there? This the blind man already knows. Eyes can tell him what the moon "looks like." They can tell him what the moon "appears to be." That the moon has an appearance, the blind man knows. But eyes cannot tell him what "goes on in the moon." To know this would require more than eyes. The blind man knows that appearances do not necessarily reveal what goes on behind them.[9] He implies that it is necessary to "come into touch" with an appearance in order to see what lies behind it and to see what makes it appear the way it does. This cannot be done with the eyes alone. Seeing may be believing, but it is not necessarily knowing. Diderot's blind man is articulating what Berger (1963, 23) calls the "first wisdom" of sociology, namely that "things are not what they seem." Eyes see only what "seems to be" (Arendt 1971, 38).

The blind man rejects the gift of eyes for a second reason: that they cease to see before hands cease to touch. Objects like the moon, when experienced only with the eyes, come and go. When objects disappear, we can keep them only through visual memory (Tausigg, 1993) and, like appearances themselves, memories fade. Touch, the blind man suggests, is another matter. Touching brings appearances *to* oneself. The self is now, literally, "in touch" with the appearance. Touching symbolizes inquiry and a coming-to-know what lies behind appearances. Touching can tell us what goes on behind appearances, and this knowledge remains with us even after appearances are "out of reach." This wisdom endures, even after memory fades and eyes cease to see.

Diderot's blind man suggests that he would be as well off perfecting the senses he has as acquiring the one he lacks. What would be more perfect than longer arms? He treats longer arms "as if"[10] they would give him something of which he is now deprived. Longer arms would bring more of the world within his reach. The blind man knows that visual objects are constantly appearing and disappearing. He seeks to know what goes on behind appearances. Perfecting his touch, not acquiring vision, is the only thing that would help him in this.

Like Diderot's blind man, Mark wishes he had longer arms. He could then find the ball. He would have the ball in his grasp and in his world. Eyes would be of no help to him in this quest. They would allow him merely to "see the ball." Eyes would not *give* the ball to Mark's world. Even if he had eyes that could see, Mark would have to move to the ball (lengthen his arms) in order to "be in touch with it." Mark's mother is able to "hand him the ball." The ball passes from her hand to his, from her touch to his. Like Diderot's blind man, Mark treats longer arms "as if" they would give him something of which he is now deprived.

Mark's conception of seeing as having "really, really, really long arms" allows him to imagine his mother possessing the ball even though it is out of his reach. This is not the case for Diderot's blind man. For him, the moon is out of reach for everyone, blind or not. Eyes can certainly see the moon, but even those who see the moon with their eyes assume that they are not seeing everything. They know that eyes need help to "see" the moon. Thus, a telescope. But this "seeing" is not something they see with eyes.

Diderot's blind man "sees" this as well. He sees that the telescope enhances the ability of eyes but does not bring objects into reach and thus does not give eyes the thing of which they are deprived. Diderot's blind man already knows that the moon is there. Eyes might refine his knowledge, and he is curious about this, but they would not give him anything of which he is now deprived; they would not put the moon "in his reach." Eyes would not "guide" him to an understanding of what goes on in the moon.

THE GUIDING TOUCH

Blind persons already know that the world is made up of appearances which are visible to eyes. The form this knowledge takes partly depends on whether a person is congenitally or adventitiously blind, but in either case blind persons often express this knowledge with the phrase, "sighted world." Coming into touch with the sighted world, however, is not achieved through a sighted guide. Getting from one place to another with a sighted guide tells blind persons nothing about what is visually "going on." That journey is out of the blind person's reach. She therefore needs a guide other than eyes.

We can see now that a blind person's search for a guide is a search for something more than the sheer ability to move through the world. That is merely one aspect of the guide. The guide must do more, or having a "sighted guide" would be sufficient. A blind person needs a guide who will not merely move her through the world but also *bring* that world *to* her and *take* her *to* it.[11] Guides bring blindness and sightedness together in a world which is neither "blind" nor "sighted" but within which they both appear and live.

The brief experience I had with Leo gave me a sense of being *taken* to the world and, at the same time, of the world being *brought* to me. This "taking and bringing" resembles the insertion into the world of which Arendt (1958, 176–178) speaks. It resembles, too, the extension or "perfection" of the sense of touch of which Diderot's blind man spoke. Leo did not "perfect" my sense of touch by making it more sensitive. I was not able, harness in hand, to touch things I had not touched before or to feel things more perfectly. Instead, my grasp on the harness handle brought the tactile character of the world closer to me and I thereby became more "in touch" with my sense of touch. Rather than "feeling" my way around the world, as I did with the white cane, my brief experience with Leo gave me an awareness of how the world expressed itself through tacticity. I was not so much *relying* on my sense of touch to get around as I was *rearranging* my sensual experience and subsequent understanding.[12]

My experience with Leo showed me just how strongly the world expressed itself tactually. I saw my remaining senses, particularly touch and hearing, taking over for my sense of sight. The sensory world would now come to me through touch, hearing, smell, and taste. Although sight was no longer a factor in my sensual experience, it remained a factor, and a key one, in my interpretation of the world; insofar as I continued to conceive of it as the "master sense," I retained the Western bias[13] that most of what we "know" about the world comes from our sense of sight. In order to continue knowing and being in touch with the world, I would have to use my remaining senses. Primarily, I would have to construct the visual appearance of an object by touching it. People who see can do this too, of course, but they are not totally dependent on it, as I am.

Although I still treat my sense of touch as an instrument capable of giving me a sense of the visual, Leo enabled me to see my sense of touch as my distance sense. The sensory world manifested itself *in* touch without regard to sight. My experience with Leo re-arranged my senses.

This re-arrangement has been referred to in terms of "sense ratio," which for Howes (1991, 20) "is perhaps best translated as 'each sense has its reason' (in both senses)." Rejecting a quantification of the senses and following the work of Ong and others, Howes (1991, 12) suggests that there are shifts "in the 'ratio or balance of the senses' as one passes from one culture to another, and within the same culture over time."

For me, the shift in the balance, or ratio, of the senses occurred when sight was no longer a key feature of my sensual experience. Blindness tipped the scale of my sense ratio in favor of my remaining senses, especially touch and hearing. Nevertheless, sight remained, conceptually if not physically, my chief organizing sense. I used touch and hearing *strictly* to deduce and imagine the world as visual. What I touched and what I heard served as signifiers for the signified—the visual—and this arrangement of senses will undoubtedly remain with me to one degree or another. My experience with Leo facilitated yet another shift as I experienced the potential of touch as a distance sense and, for the first time, experienced its potential as the chief organizing sense. The "feel" of Leo's harness did not lead to any deduction. Instead, it was *in itself* a powerful sensuality that organized my sense of touch as stable and secure. Put simply, I was more in touch with my sense of touch. The "divine logos" of which McLuhan (Howes 1991, 20) wrote resonated in my flesh as it combined with Leo's.

We can now add to Howes's contention; not only does the balance of senses shift from culture to culture and in the same culture over time, it also shifts in an individual. This shift in my ratio of senses influenced my experience of the sensory world and reorganized my understanding of my culture. Blindness "showed" me that sightedness *could* be conceived as a culture with particular ways of "looking and seeing," understanding and knowing, and with particular ways of demonstrating this to sighted others. My grasp of Leo's harness and, through it, of his contact with the world, enhanced my conception of sightedness as a culture. This is not a strange notion, even to people who see. They do, after all, look at each other and give each other "looks." Recognizing this "looking" has a cultural basis insofar as these "looks" have meaning.

Moving through the world and coming to know it depends largely upon being in contact with culture. This understanding grounds the idea that blind persons can be independent, an idea which is itself cultural in origin. That blind persons can and must make their way through the world independently is a social conception that has evolved in the last half of the twentieth century. Even though dogs are often understood as one device among many for independent mobility, there is a sense in which

they are also conceived within the paradigm of "contact with the world" which I have been discussing. Eustis
illustrated the transformative character of this contact
in 1927 when she first witnessed a dog guide team in
Germany.

It was as though a complete transformation had taken
place before my eyes. One moment there was an uncertain shuffling blind man, tapping with a cane, the next
there was an assured person, his dog firmly in hand, his
head up, who walked toward us quickly and easily, giving
his orders in a low, confident voice.

That one quick glimpse of the crying need for guidance and companionship in the lonely, all-enveloping
darkness stood out clearly before my swimming eyes. To
think that one small dog could stand for so much in the
life of a human being, not only in its usual role of companion but as his eyes, sword, shield and buckler! How
many human beings could fill those roles with the same
uncomplaining devotion and untiring fidelity? (Dickson
1942, 65–66)

Up until then, Dorothy Eustis and her colleagues had
trained German shepherds for police and military work,
but as a result of this experience she began training
dogs for guide work and subsequently founded Seeing
Eye Incorporated, the first dog guide school in North
America.

The transformation Eustis witnessed was not only complete but sudden: the dog *suddenly* transformed the blind
man's uncertainty into assurance. Eustis believed that
this transformation came from the dog being "firmly
in hand"; the dog had enhanced and extended the

man's sense of touch. The white cane had permitted only a three-point extension of contact, which did not transform his uncertainty into confidence. Head down, intermittently tapping the cane, the man seemed to Eustis to be looking for the point of contact. With the dog "firmly in hand," however, he had six points of contact and his sense of touch became his distance sense; he was, in Eustis's eyes, "transformed." Eustis characterized this transformation as the replacement of uncertainty with confidence and assurance. What she saw was the man acquiring confidence from the dog. But the transformation is grounded elsewhere. Dog firmly in hand, the six points of contact *completely transformed* the man's ratio of senses, as the distance sense shifted from eyesight to touch.

In her somewhat melodramatic rendering of the experience, the transformation Eustis witnessed allowed her to "glimpse" a blind person's "need" for a guide. For Eustis, eyesight is the guide with which human beings are naturally endowed. She conceives of the dog guide as a replacement for this natural guide; the dog becomes the person's "eyes, sword, shield and buckler," things that Eustis implicitly connects with eyesight. Moreover, the dog takes on these roles with a devotion and fidelity unequalled by any human being. The dog is as devoted to the blind person as the eyes are "devoted" to the sighted person.

Dog firmly in hand, the movement of the blind man represents, for Eustis, the natural movement of a sighted man. With the dog in hand, he moves "as if" he had the natural gift of sight. There is some truth to Eustis's interpretation, since the dog, who can see, is now acting as if she *were* the blind man's eyes. What the dog sees is now transferred to the blind man through the handle of the dog's harness; the man is now in touch with his dog's seeing eyes and has a firm grasp on the world. Diderot's blind man could only wish for longer arms. This man has acquired them. He has perfected his sense of touch and is now moving through the world *as if* he had eyes.[14]

Eustis's depiction of the dog guide as the replacement for sight contains an implicit version of independence. She says that no human being can be as devoted or faithful in the role of a blind person's eyes as a dog guide is. It is amazing to think, she says, that a dog can "stand for so much in the life of a human being." When conceived as the replacement for the natural gift of sight, the dog guide indeed stands for much—she represents the "natural state of affairs." Human beings are *naturally* endowed with sight and it is only through some "unnatural" state of affairs, such as disease or accident, that sight is disrupted. This is the disruption Eustis saw when she saw the blind man shuffling with uncertainty, tapping his white cane. When she saw the blind man, dog firmly in hand, walking quickly and easily with his head held high, Eustis saw this disruption "completely transformed" into the original and natural state of affairs.

Eustis saw the dog guide as far superior to a sighted human guide. Tireless and devoted, the dog will always respond when the blind person calls on him or her for guidance. Unlike a human being, it will not complain, and it will not tire of guiding. But this is only part of the reason for Eustis's opinion that dogs make better guides than human beings do. Their superiority makes implicit reference to a version of independence for blind persons that is tacitly framed within the distinction between a sighted guide (humanity) and dog guide (nature).

One aspect of this distinction is the understanding that thought is an essential feature of human life.[15] Human beings possess thoughts, attitudes, and conceptions regarding the social world, including attitudes toward, and conceptions of, blindness. Therefore, when sighted persons guide blind persons they do so with an interpretive set of attitudes and preconceptions regarding blindness, whether explicit or implicit. Some sighted persons conceive of blind persons as helpless and pitiful and they guide with this conception either explicitly or implicitly in mind. Others view blind persons as lacking knowledge of the world, and their guiding is informed by this preconception. Whatever the attitudes of sighted guides, their guiding is informed by these interests and often expresses them. The blind person does get from here to there, but he receives conceptions of blindness along the way. For example, I was standing at a street corner waiting for the light to change in my favor. At this point, I was still using a white cane. A man literally grabbed my arm and proceeded to "guide" me across the street. Unfortunately, he wanted to guide me in the wrong direction. The man did not ask me if I needed help; he just "helped."

Unlike dog guides, sighted guides are not *only* guides. They have a variety of other interests, activities, and responsibilities, of which guiding is only one. Blind persons can use sighted guides only when they are available. They may be too "tired" to guide or, if called on too often, they may "complain."

Eustis's understanding of sighted guides raises the idea of "dependence." In addition to being dependent on a sighted guide's time and availability, the blind person is also dependent on the guide's interpretive conceptions of blindness during the interactive process of guiding. A dog guide, in contrast, only guides, and guides only one person. Other activities—playing, sniffing, running—are secondary to guiding. The blind person is not dependent in the same way on the dog's time and energy for guiding, because that time and energy are devoted strictly to guiding the blind person. Moreover, the dog guide does not approach the blind person with a set of interpretive conceptions of blindness. The dog guides without judging. Dog firmly in hand, the blind person is independent of the interests and preconceptions of sighted guides. This is the version of independence contained in Eustis's account of the blind man's transformation.

This chapter's discussion of blindness and sightedness, guiding and the idea of independence, and the development of a distance sense not dependent on sight, lays the foundation for understanding the possibility of dogs as guides for blind persons. Dogs as guides *symbolize* a version of blindness; when most people see a dog in harness, they also see a blind person. Typically, however, they do not see this "blind person" as an individual with particular hopes and fears, likes and dislikes, anxieties and aspirations, but as a representative of the collective understanding of blindness. That is, they see their society's conception of blindness rather than an individual blind person. The dog does not share this conception of blindness, but it certainly does symbolize it. This symbolic order will be examined in the following chapters.

The next one is devoted specifically to the two-fold process of applying for a dog guide; first, the process through which an individual blind person decides that a dog is an appropriate guide, and then the process through which the staff of a dog guide school decide whether the decision of the blind person is appropriate. Blindness, guiding, and independence together weave the fabric that makes up the social construction of dog guide use. While this fabric is often visible to the "naked eye," its threads usually are not. The following chapter will attempt to bring them into view.

CHAPTER THREE
Is That One of Those Blind Dogs?

"Excuse me."
"Me? Are you talking to me?"
"Yeah, is that one of those blind dogs?"
"Jeez, I hope not. Forward, Smokie."

"Watch where you're going Carlo. That's a blind dog."

EXCHANGES LIKE THIS are common when Smokie and I move about our city or travel to different places. Despite the confusion and irony embedded in the description of Smokie as a "blind dog," it does reveal a fundamental truth: Dog guides are inexorably tied to blindness. Seeing a dog in harness brings blindness into one's field of vision. It is conceptually impossible to see a dog guide without seeing blindness.

Sometimes I am mistaken for a trainer of dog guides. While standing with Smokie at a crosswalk, a pedestrian said, "Man, you people sure do a wonderful job training those dogs." On another occasion someone said, "You must get a lot of satisfaction from training those dogs to take blind people around." Comments like these are less common than references to Smokie as blind, but both reveal the inescapable connection between dog guides and blindness.

As I have tried to describe in chapter two, I began to think about blindness in new ways when I lost the remaining 10 percent of my sight. I realized that blindness resides in *us* as much as in a white cane, in Braille, or in the physiology of the eye. All of these are part of the gestalt of blindness. Dog guides and white canes "put us in mind" of blindness and of the *meaning* blindness has for us. Of course dog guides do not *cause* blindness, but the two things *belong* to each other and *release* each other into appearance. Merleau-Ponty (1962, 50) writes,

> One phenomenon releases another, not by means of some objective efficient cause, like those which link together natural events, but by the meaning which it holds out—there is a *raison d'etre* for a thing which guides the flow of phenomena without being explicitly laid down in any one of them, a sort of operative reason. . . . To the degree that the motivated phenomenon comes into being, an internal relation to the motivating phenomenon appears; hence, instead of one merely succeeding the other, the motivated phenomenon makes the motivating phenomenon explicit and comprehensible, and thus seems to have pre-existed its own motive.

The dog guide "releases" blindness into consciousness through the "meaning" it "holds out" to experience—both the experience of the blind person using the dog and the experience of those who witness the pair in action. My decision to look for a dog guide released *my* blindness into my consciousness differently from before. The *raison d'etre* of a dog guide is the guiding of a blind person and this reason for being "guides the flow" of blindness into the world and releases it into human consciousness.

In Merleau-Ponty's terms, the "motivated" phenomenon (blindness) does not succeed the "motivating" phenomenon (dog guide). There is an "internal relation" between the two by which blindness makes the appearance of a dog guide "explicit and comprehensible." Seeing the dog *as guide* makes us see blindness as "in need of guidance." It may seem as if blindness precedes the dog guide, but blindness does not appear as a natural, physiological event. Blindness is given to experience by experience. We notice our blindness through a transformation of how and what we see. We notice the blindness of others when we see white canes, dog guides, and so on. Blindness may be understood in its physiological aspect, but this understanding comes through a "conceiving of experience" rather than as a brute natural fact.

Blindness appears in experience, as well as in consciousness, through ways of understanding seeing and not seeing that take the form of individual and collective representations. Even though blindness *seems* to precede the dog guide, the dog guide releases blindness by giving it a meaningful character, or by putting us "in mind" of blindness.

The question, "Is that one of those blind dogs?" acquires comprehensibility when the dog in harness releases both guide and blindness into experience. Interpreted literally, the question would be incomprehensible, a case of the "blind leading the blind." The

expression "blind dog" results from the dog guide's re-
leasing blindness into the world, an essential part of the
dog guide's life.

My search for a guide was also a "searching of my
blindness" that made me consider how to fill the "void"
left by the loss of my vision. I did experience a sense of
void, but it was not a vacuous sense of emptiness. A host
of thoughts and feelings rushed into this void; my experience was not the "lonely, all-enveloping darkness" that
Eustis saw before her "swimming eyes" when she looked
at the blind man. It more closely resembled the "shuffling uncertainty" that she observed.

I realized that in my "10 percent days" I had been living with a "mixed nature," a mixture of seeing and not
seeing. Although I felt an affinity with the "sighted
world," I lived in the world of blindness as well. I had one
foot in each world but belonged to neither. Once I had
lost most of my "10 percent vision" and experientially belonged to the world of blindness, I still clung to my old
identity and my affinity with the world of sight. My consideration of a dog guide, however, brought home starkly
the things I could no longer do for myself. I became pre-
occupied with a "doing self" and with an identity envel-
oped in darkness by lack of competence. This was not the
loneliness Eustis imagined, but an *aloneness* released by
an uncertain shuffling in the world.

A dog guide, I thought, might restore some of my lost
competence and confidence, which were, after all, what
"guidance" meant to me. My cry was not of loneliness, of
longing for a companion, but of one left standing alone,
betrayed and deserted by the life-long companion of
sight and the competence it bestows. This was the blindness released by my thinking about a dog guide. I could

not imagine myself shuffling uncertainly through the world; this was an identity foreign to me. I was not altogether certain that a dog guide would provide the competence I needed to return to myself. But since the white cane held out no hope, I proceeded with the application procedure for a dog guide.

LOOKING BACK

I had a very difficult route getting to and from work in the heart of London. I had so many bumps and bruises I couldn't take any more of it. I was getting so tired and stressed that I decided it was about time I got a dog. I had been very anti-guide dog. I thought they smelled, put their noses up at you and generally made a mess. Also there is a responsibility attached to having a dog. I wouldn't change that for the world now. I would never ever be without one, if I could help it.

I didn't have the confidence to use a white cane, and although I was afraid of dogs, I felt it was the lesser of two evils. As my sight deteriorated and I walked slower and slower using a white cane, I decided to get a dog. I also thought dogs broke down barriers with other people.

I was intent on a teaching career which obviously needed mobility and I hated the idea of a long cane. It was not at all feminine and it made me feel as if I looked more blind.

I was too frustrated by not being able to go out on my own, waiting for someone to take me and the family members not being able to guide me very well. They made such a song and dance about it. I found quite new freedom and independence when I got the guide dog.

My husband talked me into getting a guide dog. I was working in bad conditions, heavy traffic and living in a very bad area. I was having very bad stress-related headaches. Looking back, I must have been crazy not to have decided about it myself. (Ed and Toni Eames as cited in *Dog World*, September, 1993)

These people all had reasons similar to mine for getting a dog guide. Their comments look back from the interpretive position of the present (Berger 1963, 55) on the difficulties they experienced before getting a dog guide. Each one rejected the white cane for one reason or another, but they all knew that they needed a guide. A dog, though the lesser of two evils for some, was clearly superior to either a cane or a sighted guide. For all these people, a dog held out the best—perhaps the only— hope of freedom from stress headaches, bumps and bruises, exhaustion, travelling at a snail's pace, and the "song and dance" that comes with dependence on a sighted guide. A dog guide may be "second-best" to sight, but the people quoted above all agreed that it represented the least of all guiding evils. Like them, I hated the white cane. I felt that the white cane made me "look more blind" but, more importantly, I *felt* more blind when using it.

I approached my decision to apply for a dog guide not with the understanding that a dog was the least of all guiding evils but that it was the best of all guides. Even so, I knew that the dog guide was, without question, a replacement for my sight; and sight was certainly my preferred choice for a guide. I saw the application for a dog guide as a brute necessity, and I approached it with the sense that *any* guide would be second-best to the quintessential guide of sight.

APPLYING FOR A DOG GUIDE

The application process was more complicated and troublesome than I had expected. Like most schools in North America (Eames, 1994), the school to which I applied required that I provide a medical report, ophthalmological report, orientation and mobility report, and letters of personal reference. Securing these reports and forwarding them to the school took several months. I also had to complete a questionnaire about my experience with dogs, my attitude toward them, and my knowledge regarding their care.

1. Do you enjoy a dog following you around your home?
2. Do you enjoy a dog licking you?
3. What is the approximate cost per month of feeding a dog?
4. Have you ever owned a dog before? If so, what breed?

The form also asked whether I would take my dog guide on vacation with me, what behavior I expected from a dog guide when entertaining visitors, what I thought of playing with the dog guide, and so on. The questionnaire was obviously designed to measure my "appropriateness" for having a dog guide, and for enrollment in the school in the first place. (This questionnaire was later eliminated from the application process.)

After receiving my application, a staff member phoned to arrange a home visit, and she told me she would be bringing a dog with her. Tanya and I spent the next few days anxiously awaiting her visit and wondering if the dog was to be *my* dog. When the staff member, Sonya, showed up the next week, she had with her a yellow Labrador Retriever named Fonzy. Fonzy was not my dog, as it turned out, but a "demo-dog" used to demonstrate guide skills and to assess the appropriateness of applicants. The home visit was very casual. Sonya did not have a prepared set of questions, but I was intent on getting a dog guide and I knew there was a long waiting list at most of these schools, so I tried to present myself in the best possible light. I volunteered that I had a good teaching job (and could thus afford to feed a dog), stressed that I was physically fit and worked out regularly, and in other ways told Sonya what I thought she wanted to hear. The school accepted me, though not, I suspect, because of my comments during the home visit.

After we'd talked for a while, Sonya suggested that it was time for me to get the feel of using a dog. I made my way down the stairs and outside and waited on the sidewalk for Sonya, Fonzy, and Tanya. When they joined me, Fonzy was in his harness and Sonya was holding the leash. Sonya gave me a very quick lesson on how to grip the harness and leash and what to expect from Fonzy when he guided me around the block. She told me that Fonzy would stop at all of the curbs (down and up) and that I would have to give him directions at those points. She said that Fonzy would slow his pace if I used the command "easy" and that he would quicken it when I tapped my right leg and gave the command "hup up." In excited anticipation and some nervousness, I grasped the handle of the harness in my left hand. Sonya would be very close to Fonzy and me as we walked; I had only to give the command "forward" and we would be on our way. I turned to Tanya and said, "I can't believe this." She was just as excited and as nervous as I was. We both wanted this "demo" to be a success.

Having taken three or four steps with Leo during my visit to the school, I felt I had some idea of what to expect. But suddenly giving the command "forward" seemed filled with a significance I had not anticipated. I wondered if Fonzy would obey my commands; I wondered if I would handle him well; and I suddenly realized that people in my neighborhood—only a few of whom knew I was blind—would see me walking with a dog guide. Full of trepidation, I turned to Tanya and asked her to follow us. Then . . . "Fonzy, forward."

My worries instantly evaporated. I was conscious of nothing but Fonzy's movement in the harness and the sensation that flowed through the harness to my hand and into my entire body. I knew exactly where Fonzy was; I could feel each one of his steps, each of his four paws as they came down on the sidewalk, and this even though he was at least two or three feet in front of me. The sense of touch, strength, and balance that I had briefly experienced with Leo returned to me. As we moved briskly down the sidewalk, I smiled and closed my eyes. My nervousness seemed to flow down through and out of the harness as the magnification of touch flowed up. Eyes closed and smiling, I said "Good boy, Fonzy," loosened my grip on the harness handle, and settled back to enjoy the trip.

Fonzy began to slow our pace and a few seconds later we came to a stop. I felt in front of me with my foot, anticipating the curb but not finding it. Instead, I touched the remnants of a late winter snowbank. Another second of searching with my foot, and I found a small opening and the curb. I gave Fonzy the command "right" and we proceeded. This was one of the few times all winter long that I had not stumbled on a snowbank. We soon left the side street and turned onto a very busy avenue. Our lateral movement increased at this point. At a pace I had not experienced for years, he guided me from left to right on the sidewalk. Occasionally I would catch a glimpse of a shadow which I presumed to be pedestrians we were passing. My nervousness returned as I remembered that we were approaching a bus shelter located near the corner of a busy intersection. I had bumped into this bus shelter several times before. I wondered if Fonzy would take me around it, as bumping into it at this speed would certainly hurt. We were moving too quickly for me to know exactly where I was in relation to the bus shelter. Suddenly a dark shadow passed me on my right, and a few steps later Fonzy stopped at the curb of the intersection. We were past the bus shelter. Turning right, we headed for home.

As we approached my home, Sonya said that I could give Fonzy the command "right inside." When I did so, he turned right and stopped. I felt the stairs with my foot and, giving him the command "forward," Fonzy guided me up the stairs to the front door, where we waited for Sonya.

Once inside, Sonya handed me a treat and said that I could give it to Fonzy. I held the treat out to Fonzy but he refused it, turning his head. I was puzzled until Sonya explained that dog guides were trained not to accept food while in harness. She then removed Fonzy's harness and he gladly accepted the treat from me. I then spent a few minutes playing with him, praising him, and thanking him for our trip. Tanya could not control herself and, joining Fonzy and me, the three of us celebrated.

Sonya wanted to know what I thought of the experience. My heart was still racing with excitement and exhilaration at what I had just been through. I told Sonya I was more determined than ever to get a dog guide. The exhilarating experience I felt arriving home with Fonzy had never occurred when I arrived home with my white cane. I felt like I was celebrating and savoring the accomplishment with Fonzy, a sense of celebration that continues to this day. Even after more than five years with Smokie, we still celebrate upon our arrival home, and I still experience the same sense of exhilaration.

Sonya told us she would report the findings of her home visit to the training staff at the school and that they would make a decision within a few days. She would be in touch soon with their answer. For the next few days, Tanya and I spoke of almost nothing but Fonzy, dog guides, and how much better my life would be if I were accepted at the school. These were very anxious days. When Sonya called with the good news that I had been accepted, I was surprised to learn that there would not be a long wait. A spot had opened up in the next class and I was to begin my training in one month.

AT THE SCHOOL

"So, Gord tells me that you're going away next week to get one of those blind dogs."

"I think I'll ask for one that can see."

In the late spring of 1993, about five weeks after I had walked around the block with Fonzy, I returned to the school for the first time since the day I had met Leo and experienced my first encounter with a dog guide. Though it was only about an hour's drive from my home, the trip seemed much longer that first day. I sat quietly in the car, pondering my decision with some trepidation. I was not looking forward to the month I was required to spend at the school. Being familiar with other organizations designed to "help" blind people, I was aware of their typical institutional character, shaped usually by a conception of blindness as "helplessness" and the "we know what is best for you" attitude. The words of the staff person who compared dog guides to automobiles also echoed in my mind.

On the other hand, I was on my way to train with my new guide. Anticipating this training with both anxiety and excitement, I wondered what sort of dog the school had matched me with. I had no information about the dog's breed, gender, size, or color. Since I knew that dogs' training began when they were about fourteen months old and lasted for four to six months, I was certain that my dog would be about two years old, but that was all I knew for sure. The staff "matched" the applicant with the dog based on the written application and the home visit, and also chose a "back-up" dog for the applicant in case the first match turned out not to be appropriate. But because of the possibility that neither dog would work out, or the applicant was judged an inappropriate candidate for dog guide use, the training staff withheld the particulars of the dog guide from the student until they were sure they had made an appropriate match. For this reason, the first two days of training are conducted without a dog and are spent demonstrating the use of the harness. Students learn the commands and are told what to expect from their dog guide directly from the trainer, who simulates the dog. These two days allow the trainers to evaluate students and decide whether the match is appropriate.

When we finally arrived in the small city where the school was located, we found a restaurant and had lunch. Except for the first two days at the school, this was the last meal I was to eat in the absence of my dog guide. After lunch, we went on to the school and were shown to the room I was to occupy for the next month.

There were signs of blindness everywhere. The stairway that led to the second floor, where the rooms were located, was preceded by approximately four feet of carpeting. Other than this and a small area of the television section of the student lounge, the floors were uncarpeted, presumably so as to enhance the sound of footsteps and contribute to the ease of cleaning floors which are constantly trod on by dogs.

The rooms themselves were very spare. My small single room was furnished with a small wooden dresser that stood directly in front of the single bed. The bed was flanked by a small desk and chair. A small closet on the right and a bathroom on the left greeted you as you entered the room. The large window at the end of the room was sealed shut but, thankfully, the rooms were air-conditioned. There was absolutely nothing on the walls. Ironically, however, there was a mirror above the sink in the bathroom. As I examined my room, I asked Tanya where the telephone was; there wasn't one. I "looked around" a little longer, sat at the end of the bed, and said, "Well, at least I'll have my dog."

After much encouragement and well-wishing from Tanya and Joan, the friend who had driven us, we said our farewells. Standing there alone it seemed to me that my room was very, very blind. Only the thought of my unknown dog kept me from chasing blindly after Tanya and Joan.

I made my way down the stairs and into the main floor lounge for the first scheduled meeting, where I would meet some of the staff and the other five students in the course—three men and two women. None of us had ever used a dog guide.

Our training started in earnest the next morning. We gathered in the student lounge, where we met the two trainers who would be spending the next month teaching us how to work our dog guides. For the next two days, we attended lectures about dog care and dog guides. The trainers led us around the streets immediately surrounding the school, using a harness to simulate the way our dog guides would perform this task.

The trainers told us a little about the training of the dogs, which was done solely on the basis of reward. They corrected a dog for making a mistake only when they were certain that the dog understood what it was required to do. Only when the dogs knew the difference between left and right, which all of our dogs did, could they be corrected for making a mistake. Playing the role of the dog, the trainers taught us how to make these corrections. If the dog turned right when given the command "left," for example, a simple, sharp "no" would return the dog to the forward position. If this "no" failed, the leash was used to bring the dog back. In the extreme case where a dog would not respond even to this, we were taught how to do a "leash correction"—

snapping the leash, which tightened and then immediately loosened the choke chain—along with the "no" command. We were warned that our dogs would not immediately work as well with us as they did with the trainers.

Your dogs are going to test you every chance they get. They just want to find out what they can get away with. You have to show them who's in charge, who's boss. Remember, they're well trained. They know every command and they're all working well. But that's with us. We've trained them and they've learned to listen to us over the last few months. This has to be switched over to you now. The biggest thing is, don't let your dog get away with anything. If you do, they won't respect you. If this happens, well . . . they're just not gonna work. When you get your dogs tomorrow morning you have to spend some time with them. You have to get close and bond with them. This will happen over the next month gradually. Working them and showing them who's boss will get them to respect you and get close to you. The most important thing to remember is that they'll test you. It takes anywhere from six months to a year for a dog guide team to work well. So this next month is only the beginning of the training. You have to continue the training forever. Starting tomorrow, we're gonna teach you how to be trainers. Your dogs are trained, they know what to do—you don't. That's what you're gonna learn.

I left this meeting with the sense that whether or not I would use a dog guide effectively was up to me. The dogs were well trained. They knew what to do. Whether or not I developed a good working relationship with my dog guide would depend on my own ability to learn. Any notions I had about a dog guide being a robotically trained animal were quickly dismissed. A dog is not a car. My dog might or might not obey me, might or might not respect me, might not even like me. It was up to me to earn the dog's respect, and I would only be able to do that by allowing it to do the work it had been trained to do. This was the attitude with which I approached the next morning—the morning I met my dog.

But that afternoon, something unexpected happened. The trainers asked us to gather outside on the patio, where they told us we were going to meet all the dogs. They explained that they would not tell us which dog was matched with which student. We would just, as they put it, "get to meet all of the dogs." The trainers departed for the kennel while we sat on picnic benches awaiting the dogs.

It turned out that the dogs were just as excited as we were. The door of the kennel opened and the dogs ran toward us jumping, prancing, and licking any face that happened to be close enough. Months of being kennelled was starting to tell on the dogs and they were extremely happy to be out and meeting someone new. After the initial chaos subsided, the trainers brought each of the dogs to us in turn and introduced them. We still did not know which one of them had been chosen for us.

I was, however, given a strong hint as to which dog was mine. Although they did not admit this, I suspect that this was intentional on the part of the trainers. As he introduced me to one of the dogs—Smokie, a two-and-a-half-year-old male black Labrador Retriever—the trainer asked me to put a leash on him. "Walk him around a little, see what he's like." Smokie was big, strong, and very happy. In fact, he was exuberant, and despite my command "heel," he continually jumped up on me and licked my face. I persisted until we were finally walking together, Smokie calmly heeling at my side. He seemed very attentive, and as I walked with him, even though our only contact was a leash, I could feel Smokie's power and eagerness. I wondered how he would feel in harness. I hoped he was mine.

For the rest of that afternoon and evening, the trainers and I teased each other. I insisted that I knew Smokie was my dog. They insisted he was not, but with a lot of exaggeration and laughter. That evening I learned something of Smokie's history. Unlike the other dogs, Smokie had been in the kennel for approximately one year. His training was completed in four months, but an appropriate match for him had not been found. "Smokie's been in the kennel too long," the trainer explained. "He was becoming lethargic and a little depressed." What I heard in this story, and in the teasing, was that Smokie was my dog.

At ten o'clock the next morning, I sat on my bed in my room waiting, I hoped, for Smokie. I had turned on my tape recorder so that I could have an audio record of receiving *my dog*. The trainer called out from outside my door, "I'm here with your dog." I heard the door open and the words, "Here's Smokie." Smokie was even more exuberant than he had been the previous afternoon. He leaped on me and we rolled across the bed and down the other side.

The trainer left us alone, and we spent the next hour playing with the toys I had purchased for him. I showed him his bed, his food bowl, and the desk drawer where I was storing his treats. Smokie was especially interested in the last, and for the next month he went directly to the desk drawer whenever we returned to our room. We spent the last half hour of our first morning together on the floor, me sitting and Smokie sleeping, his head resting on my lap. At noon, I put his harness on and we proceeded first to his relief area and then to the lunch room. This was the first of countless times that I put the harness on *my* guide. I flexed my fingers gently around the harness handle and leash, and in the speaking of the very first "forward" to Smokie, I knew that my search for a guide was over and that Smokie and I would travel the world together for a very long time to come.

Toward the end of my training, when the trainer was confident that Smokie and I were a good match, he told me that I had been Smokie's "last chance." The staff had hoped that I would be able to work with Smokie, given his speed and strength, and they were happy that everything had worked out. Of course, no one was happier than I.

WHO IS SMOKIE?

Soon after my training with Smokie began, I realized that becoming familiar with his extensive vocabulary of commands was only one aspect of learning to work with him. I also had to get to know Smokie, to discover exactly who he was. In the beginning, Smokie's identity presented itself to me only through "reputation." I knew him initially as a well-trained dog guide, which was how he had been introduced to me. I "filled in" more of Smokie's identity with the plethora of assumptions and presuppositions I held about dog guides; my interaction with him was animated by my interpretation of his social identity—dog guide. I treated Smokie not merely as *a* dog guide but as *any* dog guide.

Smokie's identity as a dog guide gives him a "member-ship category" (Sacks 1972, 32; 1.1.1) that provides a means of interpreting him; it allows us to develop a set of social expectations and typifications regarding our inter-action with him. In this, Smokie's is no different from any other membership category. Similar interpretive work is at play in our relations with other people; membership categories shape our interactions with every social iden-tity, whether blind persons, doctors, lawyers, bricklayers, men, or women. We come to know one another initially through membership categories and thereby through our own particular social identities. I came to know Smokie initially through his social identity as a dog guide.

But it wasn't long before I came to know Smokie in a different way. He was still a dog *and* a guide. As much as they have been enhanced over the past five years, I still hold assumptions and presuppositions about what it means to be a dog as well as what it means to be a guide. In time, however, I came to know Smokie as an *individual* dog, with particular likes and dislikes. I learned what made him happy or unhappy, what distracted him from his work, what made him anxious, and so on. I learned very quickly that Smokie did not want to go back to the kennel. To leave the main building of the school, we had to pass through a door, down a flight of stairs, through another door, and out. At the bottom and to the imme-diate left of the stairs was the door leading to the kennel. For the first week or so, Smokie would move as far right as he could as we proceeded down the stairs. He would move as far left as possible when we returned up the stairs. Smokie was keeping as far away as possible from the door to the kennel. I realized that he wanted our relationship to work as much as I did, if for different reasons.

Smokie did work quickly. At first I thought this was merely one of his traits. I soon realized, however, that his quickness was not a "trait" at all. His quickness was an expression of who he was. Smokie liked to take charge. He was constantly anticipating my commands. For example, he would not wait very long at a curb for me to decide whether we were going left, right, or straight ahead; if I didn't give him a command within two seconds, he decided on his own. The trainers did not approve of this, and though I worked on this problem, I was not as worried about it as they were. I learned to make decisions more quickly, to "out-anticipate" him. When I was not sure which way I wanted to go, I used the command "stay" to let Smokie know this. But in general his initiative has served me well over the years. When we leave a subway train and step into an unfamiliar subway station, I have no idea where to exit. When the subway doors open I simply tell Smokie "forward," and within a second or two he "makes our way" to stairs, escalators, through doors, and out onto the street.

There were other ways in which Smokie showed me that he liked to be in charge. Very often during our training, four dog guide teams worked together with one or two trainers, which meant that there were often four dog guide teams following one another down the street. "Following" was not one of Smokie's favorite activities. He was never satisfied until the other three teams were doing the following. He would move quickly in and out of

pedestrian and dog-team traffic until he was in the lead.
Then and only then would he work more smoothly. His
pace would quicken, however, if one of the other teams
approached too closely behind us.

Some of the other dogs needed encouragement in order to work. The trainers constantly reminded the han-
dlers to "get your dog going." Smokie, on the other
hand, was "self-motivated" and always wanted to be on
the move. We often began our training sessions in a
downtown coffee shop. The trainers would work with two
teams at a time while the other two waited in the coffee
shop for their turn. "Turn-taking" was one of those human interactional phenomena that Smokie never did accept. Each time the trainers got up to take two teams out
for a training session, Smokie stood. He always assumed
it was our turn, even when we had just returned to the
coffee shop from a session. He is the same even today. In
a café or bar, Smokie still interprets any movement of my
hand to my pocket as a sign that I am paying the bill. He
has come to understand my wallet in hand as a sure indication that we are ready to go. Our trainers warned us
that there would be days where our dogs would just not
"feel like working." They rationalized this in human
terms. "You know, there's days when you don't feel like
doing anything. Well, your dogs are the same. They'll
have those days." Smokie and I are now in our sixth year
together and he has yet to have "one of those days."

Smokie enjoys working and is willing to work anytime,
anywhere. This gives me a great deal of confidence. His
own eagerness and initiative do, however, require that I
exercise caution on hot, humid summer days when he
may push himself too hard. On especially humid days
he will pant and go more slowly, but he has never refused

to work. I have to keep in mind "who he is," and so I always carry water, and I plan our routes to include air-conditioned rest stops.

All dog guides are occasionally distracted from their work. Smokie, unlike some dogs, is not distracted by smells, and he rarely sniffs at anything while he is working. Nor is he distracted by people talking to him or whistling at him on the street. Some dogs experience stress after guiding their partners through a construction site or down a particularly busy street. They become a little wary and do not work as well. Smokie, in contrast, seems to thrive in difficult working conditions. It takes something extreme to faze him—loud thunderclaps or firecrackers exploding will get his attention. More than anything, however, he is distracted by other dogs. During our training at the school, he reacted violently whenever we passed another dog. The only dogs that did not distract him were other dog guides. Several months and a lot of work later, Smokie's reaction to other dogs was minimal. He no longer reacts violently unless a dog approaches him aggressively. I always know when we are approaching or have passed a dog. Smokie seems to "rise" in his harness almost as though he is walking on his toes. But unless a dog behaves aggressively toward him, this is the extent of his reaction. The trainers invoked the concepts of "pack" and "dominance" to make sense of Smokie's reaction to dogs. During his months in the kennel, they said, Smokie was the "top dog," the leader of the pack. He was very easy to train, they explained, because he was very confident and dominant and knew what he was doing.

This is who Smokie is and this is how I came to know him during that first month we spent together at the school. His identity shifted from "membership category" to a particular dog guide for me, one with a well-defined character and personality. In a similar way, Smokie must have come to know me—first as a human being, then as someone who needed to be guided, and finally as someone who needed to be guided in a particular way. Smokie and I have come to know each other through the ever-shifting meanings of membership categories and particularity. He has certainly turned out to be my "top dog."

SEEING THE WOLF IN THE DOG

Before turning to the subject of the school's conception of blindness, let us examine its approach to the question of training, which bears directly on its overall understanding of blindness and what blindness means. The training process at the school I attended was twofold. First, there was the training of the dogs as guides, and second, the training of blind persons to work with these dogs. Let us look first at the training of dogs.

The school recognizes a need to socialize the dogs as early as possible, and has designed a "Foster Puppy Program" to begin this process. When they are approximately eight weeks old, potential dog guides are given to a "foster family" that will provide the puppy with obedience training, expose it to a variety of situations, and familiarize it with people. At twelve to fourteen months of age, the puppy is "recalled" to the school. If the young dog passes a series of tests, the dog then enters the kennel and begins the dog guide training program. If the young dog fails these tests, the "foster family" either takes the dog back as a permanent pet or the school finds him or her another home. The overall objective of the foster puppy program, according to the school's manual, is "to place puppies in a home environment so that the puppy learns to be a well-behaved citizen."

In this respect, there is little difference between a puppy and a human infant. Both require socialization in a home environment, and the ultimate objective for both is good citizenship. The difference between the two resides in the reason for socialization. The reason for socializing the human infant is usually treated as self-evident. The infant is, after all, human, and an upbringing in a human home is regarded as the normal state of human affairs. The reason that a dog receives socialization in a home environment is not quite so self-evident. Here is how the school's manual describes it.

In spite of thousands of years of domestication, the dog still behaves and reacts in a manner very similar to its wild predecessor, the wolf. Wolves live in packs and organize themselves in rank orders of dominance hierarchies that function to maintain a peaceful existence. In the canine "packing order" one individual is the leader, and the remainder establish relationships of dominance and submissiveness. Everyone knows their place. Conflicts that arise are resolved by a threat from one animal and then, usually, a submissive gesture from the opponent. Dominance ranking is determined primarily by size and strength—fighting is rarely needed, unless two individuals of equal ability are challenging each other. Higher positions permit access to resources—if a prey animal is taken by the group, the pack leader is allowed to feed first or from the best portion. Others must wait until those higher in the dominance ranking have had a chance to feed. In the wolf species, dominance ranking also determines access to mates, for the dominant male guards the females and sires the majority of the pups. Females prefer to mate with the dominant male because the pups will inherit his prowess and hopefully, grow up to be pack leaders themselves, thus producing many grand pups!

In the case of the domestic dog, his family is the "pack" and the pack has to have a leader. Puppies tend to be submissive to humans but once they begin to grow and develop their fighting ability through play, they go through a stage of "testing" your dominance. At that point, they are not serious about becoming a leader, per se, they are simply developing their skills for when they mature. Obviously, a puppy who learns that his master is boss at this age will have little trouble accepting a subordinate rank when older. When the puppy begins to mature and enters the juvenile stage, it is normal for him to challenge you as leader. This is simply because the pack needs a leader and leaders get more privileges. The challenge does not mean the dog does not love you. It is a very simple and direct power play. If he is convinced that you are a perfectly competent leader and have no intentions of letting him take over, he will be quite happy to take a lower spot in the hierarchy. A subordinate position in the pack is a far more attractive prospect to a dog than not knowing where he stands. A dog that is secure in this knowledge of its rank is a happier animal and a much more desirable and safer pet. The secret is to know how to do this.

Here we have the version of the dog that dog guide trainers bring with them when they embark upon the training process.[1] Despite thousands of years of domestication and, I might add, evolution, the dog has been unable to rid itself of its wild predecessor. The wolf tenaciously hangs on and makes an appearance in the dog that is visible in its behavior and reactions to specific circumstances. The dog's nature is a mixed one: It embodies both domestication (human society) and the wildness of the wolf (nature). The wolf is transformed from an individual animal into the quintessential interpretive category for seeing and understanding the domesticated dog. The wolf is "in-the-dog" and it makes an appearance through our interpretation of the behavior of the dog.

Training thus begins in the school's understanding of the dog's "natural inclination." Part of this inclination is "packing." Wolves, and thus dogs, live in packs. The pack is the human invention for the understanding that dogs possess a social character, that they are naturally inclined to be social and to live together in society (the pack). Indeed, this inclination is so natural that our language often expresses the contrary, as in the expression "lone wolf."

The consequence of this interpretation of pack for training purposes is found in the idea of the "leader." Like the wolf, the domesticated dog *will* pack, but its pack is now a family and the dog *expects* this "family pack" to have a leader. The dog accordingly will look for a leader and, like the wolf, will use the standards of size and strength to do so. The challenge of dog training now becomes one of adapting the standard of size and strength in the dogs' natural pack to an analogous standard in the family pack.

Trainers meet this challenge by invoking their version of the wolf's method of social organization—the dichotomy of "dominance and submission." Wolf packs need leaders and big, strong wolves take on this role simply by virtue of their size and strength. Ideas such as dominance, submission, and leadership are human inventions, and dog trainers employ them in their training methods. The trainer becomes the dominant member in the training relationship, which, from the training point of view, merely plays into the dog's natural inclination. The trainer is dominant, the dog submissive.

The school employs the social organizational framework of the wolf pack as a method for training dog guides, with the Foster Puppy Program as the first step. The objective is to produce a dog who is a "well-behaved citizen." The dog's natural inclination to pack and to obey the natural law of dominance/submission is the "nature" that trainers count on in the socialization process. Wolf packs yield well-behaved wolves while family packs yield well-behaved citizens. Both result from the human understanding that wolves and dogs are naturally inclined to pack.

Conceived as natural, the inclination to pack is a strong one. Humans often attribute human motivation to wolves as a way to demonstrate the strength of this inclination. The female wolf, for example, "prefers" to mate with the pack leader. The foster puppy manual suggests that this preference is based on the wolf's understanding of genetics. The female wolf mates with the pack leader so that her puppies will inherit the leader's traits. Many grand puppies will be produced in this way, thus perpetuating and strengthening the species. Endowing the wolf with an understanding of genetics and evolutionary theory enables human beings to explain the inexplicable workings of nature as they are exhibited in the inclination for wolves and dogs to pack.

Understanding dogs in this way provides a rationale for using them to guide blind people in the first place. Trainers believe that dogs' ability to be trained resides in their social character—in their packing nature. Learning who is dominant and who is submissive, for example, is a feature of packing. Wolves learn who is boss and what the boss requires—the privilege of eating first, the best portion of the kill, the privilege of mating. Wolves learn to submit to the leader and to find their place in the "packing order." Dogs learn the same thing. They learn who is boss and what the boss requires—in the case of the family pack, obedience. When the dog learns to submit to this requirement, to obey, he becomes a well-behaved citizen. The dog enters into a "social contract" in order to gain the privilege of family membership. The same reasoning is attributed to wolves. In order to avoid a war of all against all, wolves enter into the social contract of dominance and submission in return for the privilege of pack membership.

This version of social order is what provides for the possibility of the formation of the "bond" between dog and person. The domestication of the dog refers to the domestication of the natural inclination to pack. The human is understood as dominant and the submissive dog will learn to recognize and obey the desires of the human. If the human desire is guiding, the dog will guide. Some dogs will be better at guiding than others. Evolutionary theory is once again invoked by trainers as a way to "naturally select" for dogs who display a great capacity for guiding. Dog guide training schools often initiate their own breeding programs for such purposes and all schools test dogs for their capacity to guide.

The leader of a wolf pack demonstrates his dominance

as a way to rebut any testing of his leadership; this, the theory goes, minimizes conflict in the pack. Dog guide trainers use the same rationale when they tell blind persons that their new dog guides will "test" them, and that they must show the dog "who's boss." The wolf pack leader's demonstration of his dominance also serves as a lesson to young wolves in how to grow into a "well-behaved" adult. Dominance is understood as the primary method of socialization through which the dog learns the skills of citizenship. But more than the acquisition of skills, dominance is employed by pack leaders, both wolves and trainers, to impart the *value* of pack life to neophyte wolves and "dog citizens."

It follows, given an appropriate level of capacity, that the dog can learn many things, even how to guide a blind person. Learning citizenship is a result of socialization, whereas learning how to guide a blind person is the result of training. In an analogous way, the young wolf is socialized to be an appropriate pack member but is "trained" to bring down a caribou.

For both the trainer and the blind person, the establishment of dominance is tantamount to asserting and demonstrating "pack leadership." The dog will submit to dog guide training only if the trainer is perceived, first, as part of the pack and, second, as pack leader. The dog guide will submit to guiding the blind person only if that person is perceived in the same way.

The comparison of the dog with the wolf, along with its pack theory and its notion of dominance and submission, suggests that the dog guide "partnership" is one steeped in dominance, with the blind person being unquestionably the dominant partner. I was told that I needed to "stay on top of Smokie at all times." Smokie was "definitely the leader of the pack," according to the trainer, "a dominant, hard dog." I had to "show him who's boss." All of the students were given this admonition in one way or another.

The trainers gave us another admonition, however, even more frequently and forcefully. Over and over again we were told, "Follow your dog!"—an admonition that seemed to contradict "Show your dog who's boss." What were we to make of this contradiction?

FOLLOW YOUR DOG

"Follow your dog" is not an unintelligible piece of advice when learning how to work with a dog who is trained to guide you. But "showing your dog who's boss" while following his lead is less comprehensible. Since Smokie is a dominant dog, it is necessary for me to show him "who's boss." But as the one being guided, I must follow him. At times, I am the boss; at other times, Smokie is. A blind person can follow a dog only when it is understood that being the boss (pack leader) is a position *shared* with the dog. A clear-cut distinction between dominance and submission may be useful in making sense of wolf behavior, and be extended to the training of dog guides, but the distinction becomes somewhat blurred in the dog guide/blind person partnership.

Rigid attempts to enforce this abstract distinction often spell trouble for the dog guide team. I experienced such trouble the very first time Smokie and I worked together. On my first trip out of the school building, I was instructed to proceed to an open field located behind the kennel. I was familiar with this route from my first two days at the school. Smokie's harness in hand, I proceeded out of the building and turned left toward the field. Suddenly, Smokie began moving right. Knowing that the sidewalk went straight to the field, I guided Smokie back to the left. The trainer, who was behind me, instructed me to tell Smokie to stay. He then asked me, "Does the word 'guide' in 'dog guide' mean anything to you?" He then explained that Smokie was guiding me around a pylon that he had placed in the middle of the sidewalk.

This experience, however, was not enough to teach me to follow my dog. Later that week, I encountered a much more serious form of trouble. Smokie and I were walking down a street at our usual fast pace. The trainer, as usual, was following some distance behind us. At one point, Smokie began to veer left. Thinking he was making a mistake, I did not follow. At that precise moment, I collided with a parking meter, feeling the full force of the collision in the middle of my chest. My first response was to attend to Smokie. I was concerned that he might have been hurt. I felt the pain of the collision as soon as I discovered that Smokie was fine. The trainer was on the scene in a few seconds. After asking me if I was all right, he suggested that in the future I should remind Smokie of what I had run into by saying, "Post, Smokie, post," and tapping it with my hand. He suggested that I keep this in mind "especially if you are not going to follow your dog." The trainer had seen the collision coming, but because I was in good physical condition—and because I was having difficulty following the admonition, "Follow your dog"—he had thought it best to let the collision occur. From that point on, to this day, I *follow* Smokie.

Following your dog requires a re-working of the

dominance/submission dichotomy. The dichotomy is a human abstraction used to make sense of wolf, and therefore dog, behavior. Dominance and submission are ideas that human beings bring to their observations of animal behavior. The concept of the "pack," for example, derives from social ideas we bring to observing wolves. That wolves and dogs live in packs and are social animals is undoubtedly true. But it may also be true that they have ways of organizing their experience other than pack behavior. We will never have full access to the way a dog's mind works, and so we rely on abstract concepts like these.

Theories of dominance and submission are less fruitful for a dog guide team than for other types of animal observation and interaction. Blind persons must learn to work their dogs effectively and to care for them. The dog must be brushed, bathed, its ears cleaned, its teeth brushed, even though it may balk at this. The dog must submit to human corrections and human care. In other situations, however, the dog must have control, or dominance. If parking meters are to be avoided, the person must follow the dog. If the dog stops and refuses to move, the person must determine if there is something dangerous in the way. The person must submit to the dog in these situations even though it is tempting to *think* that she or he knows better. Learning to be flexible about dominance and submission is the quintessential requirement in an effective and mutually respectful dog guide team. For blind person and dog guide, leadership is not a static or immutable position held only by the human partner but something dynamic and fluid that flows from one partner to the other and back again—a relationship of trust flowing freely through the harness in both directions. They lead and follow one another through the world, moving as one. In this movement, they discover their world, come to understand it, and graciously meet any challenges and opportunities the world holds out to them. They make this world "their world."

The one new feature of the pack that Smokie and I now formed was blindness. It was essential that Smokie and I incorporate blindness into the bond we were developing together. Even though the trainer had trained Smokie from the point of view of blindness, it was only a point of view. Smokie now had to lead, and be led by, a "real" blind person. His task was not merely to guide me but also to provide me with independence. His former pack leader was independent of blindness; I was not. The trainer "saw" Smokie guiding; I needed to "feel" him doing so. Smokie's guidance had to make me "feel" independent. Feeling independent meant I needed to depend on Smokie's natural inclination and learned ability to guide.

This more fluid understanding of dominance, submission, and leadership presupposes the dog's inclination to enter into such a relationship. Without that inclination, it would be impossible for dogs to guide blind persons at all. And while such an inclination may be framed in "natural" terms, it can also be conceived as a virtue. Aristotle drew a connection between "natural inclinations" and "virtue." He says,

> Intellectual virtue in the main owes both its birth and its growth to teaching (for which reason it requires experience and time), while moral virtue comes about as the result of habit . . . from this it is also plain that

none of the moral virtues arise in us by nature; for nothing that exists by nature can form a habit contrary to its nature. For instance the stone which by nature moves downward cannot be habituated to move upwards, not even if one tries to train it by throwing it up ten thousand times . . . nor can anything else that by nature behaves in one way be trained to behave in another. Neither by nature, then, nor contrary to nature do the virtues arise in us. (*Nichomachean Ethics*, Book Two, 15- 25)

Conceding to the wisdom of contemporary culture, we may say that "working with blind persons" is a virtuous occupation. If we further concede that a dog guiding a blind person is engaged in work—that the dog is a "working dog"—it follows that the dog guide, too, is involved in a virtuous occupation. Trainers use repetition and reward as the primary techniques for training dogs for guiding work. Dogs learn to guide when trainers repeatedly take them through the tasks required, until that work becomes habitual. If work with blind persons is virtuous and if a dog guide is understood as working with blind persons and learns to do so as a result of habituation, it follows that a dog guide, in Aristotelian terms, possesses "moral virtue."

The end to which dog guide training aims may now be understood as the inculcation of virtue in a dog. Dogs do not, by nature, guide blind persons; this virtue is the result of habituation achieved through training. But a dog can *only* be trained to develop the habit of guiding a blind person through the understanding that there is nothing in the nature of a dog that is contrary to such a habit.

BLINDNESS AND THE SCHOOL

Like most dog guide training schools, the one I attended was residential. Conventional wisdom in the field of dog guide training holds that it takes approximately a month for a blind person to bond with and to learn how to work the dog. The residential program permits the blind person to focus solely on this objective without the distractions of home life. The intention of the school is to return a blind person home with the fundamentals of dog guide work and the beginnings of a bond with the dog. Their relationship is expected to continue to grow throughout the life of the dog guide team.

But the residential requirement has another consequence which is largely unintended. The school must organize itself in a way that will accommodate blind residents. This organization is accomplished through the school's conception of what blindness is and of what blind persons need in order to live in the school for a month. The unintended consequence is that an image of blindness is organizationally produced. The way in which a school organizes and administers its residential program reveals a particular understanding of what blindness means.[2] Let us now take a closer look at the school I attended.

The residence was self-contained and located on the second floor of the school building. The rooms as well as the large hallway separating them were bereft of any decoration. The walls and floors were bare. None of the student rooms had a telephone. A trainer was on duty twenty-four hours a day and those trainers who worked evenings and nights occupied a room on this floor. This room was carpeted, decorated, and had a telephone.

The parts of the school accessible to the public were also decorated. The reception area was located in the middle of the ground floor. The offices, dining room, and entrance to the dogs' relief area were located on one side of the reception area while the student lounge occupied the other. With the exception of the television area of the student lounge and small area in front of the stairs, the school was not carpeted. There were pictures and posters in all areas of the ground floor. For example, one of the dining room walls displayed a large collage of pictures of all the classes the school had graduated since its inception in the early 1980s. The basement floor of the school was occupied by the kennel and kennel-related areas such as the quarantine room. Some office space was also provided for trainers in this area. This location was not accessible to the public.

The student lounge was used in various ways. It contained a pay telephone booth for student use. Along with the television area, the lounge had a designated smoking area. A large boardroom-style table and chairs located at one end of the student lounge were used for meetings to inform students of dog care issues and related subjects.

One image of blindness created by the physical setting is directly related to the conception of blindness as lack—as the inability to see. The style of decoration was oriented to this conception. Since the residential area was occupied by blind students, wall decorations were irrelevant. They were, however, relevant on the main floor which was accessible to a "seeing public." Since all staff members at the school were sighted, these decorations were relevant to them as well. The floors were uncarpeted because of the heavy flow of dog traffic and the notion that blind persons can glean more information from bare floors, which amplify sound.

The kitchen occupied a small area at one end of the dining room and was "out of bounds" to students and their dogs. Most of the space in the dining room held tables and chairs where students and staff ate their meals. A large refrigerator, containing soft drinks and juices for purchase, stood just outside the kitchen door. A table containing coffee was also located in this area.

What surprised me most about the dining room was the way in which meals were organized. On the first day, we were assigned specific tables and chairs where we were expected to sit throughout the month at the school. A cook prepared our meals and the trainers served them to us. They also poured our beverages. If, during the meal, a student desired more food or drink, she or he had to ask the trainer for it. The trainers also ate their meals in the dining room, and when requested would rise from their meal to accommodate student requests.

Four of the six members of our class objected to such treatment. We took our objection to the assistant executive director, explaining that such treatment fostered dependence and was demeaning both to us and to the trainers. Several meetings later, the practice was changed. Midway through the third week, the food and beverages were arranged cafeteria-style on a long table near the kitchen. Except for two students, everyone "helped themselves." Interestingly, the school has not continued this practice. Trainers were once again serving students during the very next class later that year.

There was an overall patronizing attitude toward blind

persons at the school. No alcohol was permitted and students were prohibited from leaving the school grounds unless accompanied by a trainer. Rules such as these are, in part, a result of the institutional character of residential schools. Nonetheless, they created a "children's camp" atmosphere and did little to promote an environment conducive to the training of adults.

Training sessions with students were often interrupted by impromptu meetings called by the administration. As we were about to leave the school for our morning training session, trainers would often be called to a meeting. Students would then return to the lounge and wait, sometimes for hours. On many occasions, two trainers would work with four students and their dogs. We would all get into the school van and drive to the area in which we were to work. Meetings were often called moments before we left. Again students waited, this time in the van.

The school bore all costs for all aspects of the training program. These included transportation costs for the students to and from the school, room and board at the school, dog training costs, and even the cost of the dog, including food during the month of training. Except for personal expenses, students contributed nothing financially to their training program. However, students never "own" their dogs since ownership of them remains with the school.

The school's primary source of funding is the service club, a fact that occasionally entered the routine of the training program. For example, our class attended a fundraising picnic one Sunday afternoon. We, with our dogs, were examples of the school's good work. We were paraded through the large crowd of service club members and lined up, dogs obediently sitting at our sides, to face the audience. One by one we were introduced to the approving applause of the service club. We were "proof" of the "good" their funding did. As one club member said to me,

You know, it's good to see the end product. We hardly ever get to see what our work does. It's really inspiring! To see what you people do with those dogs is amazing. It's good to know, you know, it's just great that we can make your life better. It sure is nice for us to see that once in a while.

For the most part, both trainers and students treated these occasions as a necessary evil. We dealt with the generally patronizing attitude of the service club by ourselves raising the idea of "good work," but we spoke of this in relation to our dogs.

The organization of the school, including its funding arrangement, was based on the understanding of "good work." Following the landmark work of Eustis and her colleagues, the school had a long tradition of providing dogs as guides for blind persons—of doing "good work." This orientation to work is undoubtedly "good," though it does turn on the conception that blind persons need help. In and of itself, this conception is non-problematic. Blind persons *do* require help. The problematic character of this conception resides in how the relationship between blindness and help is understood. The question is, "What sort of help do blind persons need?" If the answer is "dog guides," then the question becomes, "How should this help be provided?"

The most common way is through institutionalization—a residential school. Institutionalizing help in this way simultaneously institutionalizes blindness insofar as a conception of blindness must be evoked which will meet the self-preservation needs of an institution. For example, the school I attended organized meal times in relation to a "normal" working day. Breakfast was served (to students, literally) at eight A.M., lunch at twelve P.M., and dinner at five P.M. This schedule made it easier for the administration to organize staff. The school employed a "skeleton staff" on weekends, evenings, and nights. There was always one trainer at the school at these times. Kennel staff were present on the weekends and evenings, but not overnight. Administrative staff were present only during the nine-to-five hours of the working week.

The organization of the school was oriented primarily to meeting its institutional needs. Student needs were not an organizational priority and we had little influence on how the school understood and organized itself. Where organizational and student needs conflicted, as when an administrative meeting and student training session were scheduled at the same time, the administrative meeting always won out. Many students met with staff to suggest alternative forms of organization. Despite the friendly nature of these meetings, these suggestions were ignored, with the exception of the temporary change in the serving of meals. Students found that their residential rules were, for the most part, impossible to follow. Staff tacitly acknowledged this by turning a "blind eye" to the regular breaking of the rules.

Organizationally, the school I attended conceived of blind persons not as a "consumer group," but as a "client group."[3] This conception of blindness created an organizational structure that treated blind persons as dependent. It also permitted the school to organize itself on the basis of bureaucratic self-preservation and management. The school's conception of the dogs was also influenced by the equation of blindness with dependence. Even though the dogs were described as "guides," they were actually thought of more as "mobility devices." The school stressed the safety and efficiency aspects of work with dog guides. It also emphasized that students should play with their dogs when they were not working. But the two— serious work and the fun of play—were seen as separate activities. Nonetheless, at least two of the students in my class had fun working their dogs.

The month at the school was made tolerable by the dogs. Smokie was with me for all but the first two days of the month. We grew closer to one another each day we spent together. Because our home was relatively close to the school, Tanya visited us once or twice a week even though the rule was "visitors only on Sundays." These visits not only made the month pass more quickly, but they allowed Tanya and Smokie to get to know one another. After the first visit, Smokie "made the connection" that Tanya and I were connected. He was always very excited when Tanya visited. On one occasion Smokie and I were in the relief area as Tanya arrived. She said that she did not want to bother us and went upstairs to wait for us. Smokie was almost uncontrollable. He whined and cried as Tanya disappeared through the door. Finally I gave up and we went to my room. The three of us then returned to the relief area where he "peed in peace."

Some staff as well as students objected to the shortcomings of the school. For these staff, it was also the dogs that made these shortcomings tolerable. I did not know it at the time, but Smokie guided me through that one-month residential requirement.

The month Smokie and I had spent at the school defined our relationship in a particular way. During that month we became connected by the link of "training," which necessitated the formation of a bond. On the day before our class was to go home, the executive director of the school gave us his parting words.

> If you think you were training in the last month, it has just started for you. The training of your dog will last for the rest of its life. You're trainers now. It'll take six months to a year for you and your dog to work well together. So, if you think the training's been hard up till now, you're just starting. When you get home, it's really gonna get hard.

"Going home" meant that after a month of preparation, Smokie and I were now beginning our training relationship in earnest. Smokie would continue to guide me *if* I continued to train him. The executive director added, "They're just dogs, you know. If you don't keep up their training, they'll forget."

I was now ready to leave; I had arrived at the school as simply "me," but I was leaving as "we," as part of a dog guide team. My identity was now inexorably tied to nature and Smokie's identity was similarly tied to humanity. We were expected to nurture and strengthen our bond through the training relationship. I was a blind person in need of a guide and Smokie would fulfill this need if I continued to train him. I was a dependent blind person and Smokie would provide me with a measure of independence in return for care, love, and control. Like the scientist who tries to understand, predict, and control nature, I would have to try to understand, predict, and control Smokie. I knew that this would be a never-ending process.

Going home meant more than a change in physical locale. We were going to where I worked, played, loved, laughed, and cried, to where I *lived*. Smokie would now be a part of my life. Tanya and I lived in a neighborhood with its own particular geography, both physical and social. We shopped there, frequented its cafés and restaurants, and conducted all sorts of other business in it. Friends, enemies, strangers, and acquaintances filled our neighborhood. Smokie was about to become a part of that neighborhood, about to be immersed in my life, the life of a blind person. "Going home" meant that Smokie and I would lead and follow one another through a life in which blindness was an essential feature.

The month at school prepared me for Smokie to guide me from here to there and back again, but I was not prepared for what I would *learn* from Smokie during these trips. Smokie educated me; he guided me out of ignorance in many ways. He guided me through and simultaneously taught me about my environment. More importantly, Smokie taught me about my blindness, about its various meanings and their expressions. He simply insisted on a particular conception of blindness while we worked, teaching me that independence was not a high enough standard. Smokie guided me to aspire to a graceful independence.

The school did not prepare me for the education I was about to receive. I want now to give you a glimpse of Smokie—the teacher.

CHAPTER FOUR
The Grace of Teaching

"You'll really be living in a glass house now.
You'll get more attention than you ever
wanted."

—TRAINER AT A GUIDE DOG SCHOOL

I CAME HOME from the school as one transformed.
I had left home a blind person; I returned as a member of a dog guide team. This is when my education
really began. Until then, the relationship between me
and Smokie had revolved around the training concepts
used by the school, but now I began to learn directly
from Smokie, and I realized that the training I had received was only the starting point of our relationship.
When I saw how much Smokie had to teach me, our
relationship acquired a new and unexpected "tone"
(Van Manen 1986).

Before I address this new tone, let me describe the
home to which Smokie and I returned. This will make
the distinction between training and teaching clearer
and will prepare the way for an understanding of how
independence springs from the grace of teaching.

HOME AT LAST

Before we students left the school with our new dogs, the trainers reminded us that our presence in our neighborhoods would now be much different. Whereas my neighborhood had experienced me and only me, it would now experience me as "two," as a dyad, to use Simmel's term (1950, 118–144). My new "dyadic identity" would make me more visible than I had ever been before. In the words of one trainer,

> Remember, no matter where you go in your neighborhood people will notice you. Everyone is going to talk to you. You'll meet people you never met before. You'll really be living in a glass house now. You'll get more attention than you ever wanted. You'll get a rep in your neighborhood. This is sometimes hard to deal with, so you should be aware that it's going to happen.

In their way, the trainers were telling us that we were returning home not merely with a dog guide, but with a new identity. We would now be "identified" with our dogs. Although we would be noticed as two, we would be identified as one, and this new social identity would require development in our neighborhoods.

Sociologically speaking, my neighborhood is working class and largely Italian. The business sector is made up predominantly of Italian cafés, restaurants, markets, and shops. People use the cafés and bars more as places to "hang out" than as drinking or eating establishments. Italian is the "first language" of my neighborhood, and the streets are very active and lively. The many outdoor markets give the place a European atmosphere.

Even though Smokie and I have lived here for a number of years and are very familiar with the area, its social and physical environment does not permit us to daydream as we move through it. People often park their cars in typical European fashion—on the sidewalks. The outdoor markets mean that people shop on the sidewalks, which makes for an atypical pedestrian traffic flow. The essentially European make-up of the neighborhood attracts many tourists. All of this means that moving through our neighborhood is very challenging for Smokie and me. Smokie seems to thrive on the challenge and he guides me through our neighborhood with a speed my blindness never permitted me before.

Because I had frequented these markets, cafés, and other establishments before I had Smokie, I knew many of the proprietors and patrons. But I knew these people within the social context of "customer" and had only a "distant familiarity" with them. We recognized and greeted one another but not, in most instances, by name. Because I did not use a white cane and was not in the habit of disclosing it, relatively few people knew that I was legally blind.

Few people knew that I had been away at a dog guide school, and those who had noticed my absence assumed that I was away on one of my many trips. My return from this particular trip, however, was different. People in the neighborhood were not only surprised that I now suddenly had a dog guide, many of them were also surprised that I was "suddenly" blind. Before I left for the dog guide school, my vision was, in ophthalmological terms, "hand movements at three feet." I had lost even more vision during my month at the school.

Some people expressed their surprise about my "new" blindness and new dog guide to me directly while others expressed it to my partner (the human one). On the day I returned home, Smokie and I made our way to one of the neighborhood convenience stores, where the proprietor welcomed me home and I purchased an item and left. The next time Tanya was in the store, the proprietor told her that he was "totally shocked" to learn I was blind, and when Tanya explained that I had been blind for many years, he was even more shocked. He suggested to Tanya that things would be better for me now that I had a "seeing-eye dog."

On subsequent trips to the convenience store, my interactions changed dramatically. The proprietor, Joon, and I became much more personal with one another. We spoke of my blindness and of the difference Smokie was making in my life. "Now" that I was blind, Joon helped me with all the shopping I did at his store and I was able to purchase many more items than before. He often joined Smokie and me for a cappuccino at the outdoor café next door, and we began to develop a friendship. It seemed that blindness brought us closer. Joon now related to me as a blind person, something I had not permitted before.

The next few months were like an orientation course for the people in my neighborhood. I was continually answering questions about blindness and dog guides. I was also asked to explain past behavior. Some people knew that I was a writer and a teacher, and now they wanted to know how I did it. They also wanted to know how I had managed to get around.

After learning about dog guides, some people even took on the role of educating others. Soon after returning, for example, I was hanging out in a neighborhood bar with a new friend named Celia. I had met her when Smokie and her dog Sparkie struck up an acquaintance of their own one day at a neighborhood school yard. Tanya and I were playing with Smokie when a Golden Retriever bounded up, followed by a woman yelling "Sparkie, come!" Smokie and Sparkie liked each other immediately, and Sparkie's owner, Celia, joined Tanya and me while the dogs played. This was the beginning of a new friendship for Smokie as well as for Tanya and me, and Celia learned much about dog guides in the following weeks.

As Celia and I sat in the bar, a stranger came in, saw Smokie, and approached as if to pat him. Celia stopped him. "Don't touch him," she said. "You can't touch him. See that, it's a harness. That means he's working. Don't touch him." This sort of public education occurred frequently and continues to this day.

No matter where I went with Smokie during those first few months, people asked about him. Along with the typical comments on his intelligence and questions about training, both his and mine, everyone asked his name. Before long, everyone in the neighborhood knew Smokie. Not everyone, however, knew my name. In fact, both Smokie and I were often referred to as "Smokie."

Tanya and other friends tell me that people always watch Smokie and me as we move through the neighborhood. Some even stop what they are doing to stand and stare. Some stand perfectly still, without speaking, as I walk by. Others offer advice: "The light is green." "There's a post." "There's a car coming." Still others try to anticipate where Smokie and I are going and attempt to help. "Are you going to Gulietta's? The door is right here." "Here Smokie, here's the market." Some ask questions as Smokie and I walk by, others make comments; some speak among themselves about us. Since I've had Smokie, I am never alone in a neighborhood bar, café, or restaurant. Someone always comes up to us. They first greet Smokie and then speak with me. This was the tenor of our first few months together, anyway. Since then, though people still greet us in bars and cafés, they very rarely ask questions while we are working. Very few people touch Smokie while he is in harness—Celia has made sure of this. No one tries to help us any longer and we are not often told when traffic lights are in our favor. We have developed a reputation as competent, and we are known for our speedy pace, which is in fact the source of frequent jokes. One day I was sitting in a café with my friend Gord, when someone asked him where the wine store was. Gord gave him directions and said that it was about a ten-minute walk, adding, "unless you're these two— then it's only a two-minute walk."

Like everyone else in the neighborhood, Smokie and I now live with a reputation. Unlike the more general reputation we have in other parts of the city—"dog guide and blind person"—in our neighborhood we are "Smokie and . . . that blind guy." We are often compared to other dog guide teams, and I am compared to other blind people, Smokie to other dog guides. Comparisons are always in our favor and we are always better than any other dog team anyone has ever seen, even if the person doing the comparing has never seen another team.

Smokie and I are part of the neighborhood in two ways: We "belong" to our neighborhood not just in the sense that, like everyone else, we live there, but also in the sense that our neighbors consider us "theirs." We have become one of the "attractions" of the neighborhood, a neighborhood "establishment." Smokie and I are the "neighborhood dog guide team." We are especially part of two or three cafés and bars; Gulietta's, for example, came to be my "writing café." I use a Dictaphone, and during one of my writing sessions at Gulietta's, I overheard a conversation between Tony, the owner, and another patron.

> Patron: Boy, that's a great dog.
> Tony: No, no, don't go over there. Don't bother him; he's writing.
> Patron: He's what?
> Tony: Yeah. That's not a cell phone. That's how he writes. He's blind, you know.

Tony's warning had nothing to do with touching Smokie, but everything to do with me as a "blind writer."

At another local hangout, Smokie became a "prophet." We had been there several times together and Smokie was known and admired by the staff. Then one day, Smokie refused to enter this bar. I had no idea what was wrong. There was some construction on a sewer line down the street, but I knew that this would not affect Smokie. I made Smokie enter the bar; once inside he trembled with fear and immediately wanted to leave. I was extremely puzzled and so was Silvio, the owner of the bar. Silvio was so affected by Smokie's fear that, in traditional Italian fashion, he arranged for a priest to perform an exorcism! Soon afterwards, Smokie's fear disappeared—

but so did the construction on the sewer line. It is possible that with his superior sense of smell he had detected some sewer gas, but this is only a guess.

In many ways, our individual reputations have become moulded into one. People say that Smokie and I suit each other; some even think we were "meant for each other." We are both considered very speedy and very intense; many people say we have the same personality. There are even those who say that Smokie and I look alike! People often confuse our names. As one of my friends put it, "You guys are two in one."

This is the quintessential reputation of a dog guide team. We are a team, a dyad; we are "two-in-one." This two-in-one concept, in some ways, is not unique to Smokie and me. Good friends or intimates are often seen as two-in-one. They are two people who "belong" with each other by virtue of their relationship and how it is perceived by others. At the same time, of course, they are also separate individuals, separateness being a necessary precondition for relationship in the first place. But for Smokie and me, things are somewhat different. Unlike a relationship between two human beings, ours is animated by the distinction between human and animal, society and nature. We are "man and dog." Like society and nature, we are different from each other but interdependent. In terms of our social identity—blind person and dog guide—we cannot be separated. *My* self is now *our* self. Smokie's self too is *our* self. We are "at home together," which means that we are continuously making a home for our self. This "home-making" manifests itself in a web of social relations that identifies blindness as a feature, but an undesirable one, of home.

HOME-MAKING

Arriving home with Smokie represented much more than my coming home with a dog. After all, people come home with new pets all the time, and there follows a period of socialization. Puppies, for example, must be trained to fit into home life. They must learn not to relieve themselves indoors, not to chew on certain objects, to eat appropriate foods at specified times. The puppy must become familiar with the everyday round of home life. It must learn when and where to sleep and get used to being home alone when its humans are required to be elsewhere. The puppy must learn to accept its subordinate position in a human household. In short, it must become a "well-behaved citizen."

Smokie's arrival at home, however, was much different from a new puppy's arrival. He was already a well-behaved citizen, and he and I were already well on our way in the development of a relationship—we knew each other. Above all, Smokie did not arrive in my home as a pet, but as my guide. He had already been trained not to relieve himself indoors or chew on things, and he did not have to learn to be left alone, since he and I would always be together. He did not have to be socialized or trained as a new puppy, but rather familiarized with his new home and routine.

My goal during those first few days at home was to familiarize Smokie with every aspect of his new home. Together with Tanya, we investigated every nook and cranny of every room. We showed him where he would eat, sleep, where his water bowl would be, and so on. We explored the yard together and showed Smokie his new relief areas. One of the more important things that Smokie had to get acquainted with was the presence of our two cats, Jessie and Sugar. Although there had been a cat in the kennel at the school, I had no idea how Smokie would react to them. Tanya and I decided to feed the cats in Smokie's presence as a way to drive home to him the fact that Jessie and Sugar belonged. Given Smokie's love of food, we were a little nervous about this. I asked him to heel and sit while Tanya fed Jessie and Sugar. Though he drooled, Smokie sat obediently and watched. When the cats had finished their meal, we allowed Smokie to lick out their bowls, a practice that continues to this day.

Next, Smokie and I explored our neighborhood. I showed him everything. We went to all of my favorite haunts—to bars, cafés, and restaurants. I showed Smokie the markets in which we would shop, the bank we would go to, the route to the streetcar stop and subway station, and I introduced him to his veterinarian. Most importantly, or so it seemed to Smokie, I showed him the two schoolyards in our neighborhood where he could play and run off leash. In less than a week, Smokie was completely familiar with my home and neighborhood. He was already hesitating at the doors of familiar establishments to find out whether that was where I wanted to go. My home was now *our* home.

In our first week there, I was surprised to discover that I too was becoming more familiar with my neighborhood. I was already familiar with the streets I walked most often, and though I did not often have occasion to leave my more immediate surroundings, I knew the general area in which my neighborhood was located. As Smokie and I walked this area, however, I soon gained a new and more intimate knowledge of it.

I also became more familiar with those streets I already knew, as Smokie showed me stretches of grass, bushes, hedges, and trees that I had not been aware of. Smokie used these places as rest stops or breaks. As we walked down a street, Smokie would move quickly in one direction and stop. I would then locate the edge of the sidewalk and inevitably find some grass, trees, or other sorts of flora. I would remove his harness and he would guide me through these areas using just his leash. We now have many such stops throughout our city.

I also knew the location of the neighborhood schools, but here, too, Smokie showed me more of the property surrounding them. I became familiar with each and every corner of the bars and cafés in my neighborhood, and Smokie showed me the tables in these establishments that held the most space for him to lie down beside me. As we walked through the length and breadth of our neighborhood in that first week, I became familiar with it in ways I had never been before.

I also realized that while I was working with Smokie, I was not thinking about my blindness. I did not even feel blind. Smokie's presence was a clear and distinct symbol of blindness. I had never before had such a constant and consistent mark of my blindness, but for the first time I did not feel the negative social impact of such a mark. This remains the case to this day, even on those occasions when, because of ignorance or stupidity, we are refused entry into a public place. During those first few days with Smokie, I experienced an overwhelming sense of competence. Nothing stood in the way of our movement.

Whereas in the past I had avoided construction areas and dangerous intersections, I now sought them out with a sense of adventure. My blindness presented no barrier to Smokie's confident movement, or to our mutual enjoyment of moving together through the neighborhood.

Smokie and I were familiarizing each other with home and neighborhood, in this way making it ours. But there was one home that Smokie was re-making by himself. He was beginning to make me feel *at home* with my blindness.

Before discussing this idea of "home" in more detail, there is one more thing with which Smokie had to become familiar. Five months after Smokie and I came home, Tanya decided to acquire her own dog, an eight-week-old female black Labrador Retriever she named Cassis. There had been times in those first few months when dogs did visit our home. Smokie was very happy to see them, but these dogs always left. Cassis, however, stayed. Even though Smokie was happy to play with her for the first hour after her arrival, he was somewhat surprised that she was not leaving. It took him a week to get the idea that Cassis was staying for good. When Cassis was about ten months old, Tanya began training her to guide. Cassis learned quickly, in part, we thought, because she was able to observe Smokie. Even though Tanya is not blind, Cassis guides her as if she were.

Sometimes Tanya and I, dogs in harness, walk through our neighborhood. Everyone knows that Tanya is not blind, but they admire both her ability as a trainer and Cassis's ability to guide. Tanya does not work Cassis more than once or twice a week but even this has given her a deeper appreciation of what Smokie does for me. Tanya is also becoming more at home with blindness.

HOME AWAY FROM HOME

Blindness does separate one from the homeland of sight-edness. The only connection between blindness and sightedness occurs by virtue of, first, their oppositional relation, and, second, their co-existence in a natural and social order. This connection, however, does not guarantee that blindness and sightedness will be at home with one another, nor does it guarantee that blindness, in light of the conception that sightedness is "naturally" the homeland, will find a home.

The typical way that blind persons establish themselves "at home" is to adapt and adjust to the natural and social order by understanding that order as the "sighted world." Thus, "being at home with one's blindness" typically falls under the rubric of the "acceptance-adaptation-adjustment" paradigm. It is to establish a home which is essentially outside of, and away from, the homeland of sightedness.

In his analysis of the "exile," Said (1990, 365, 366) comments that:

> We take home and language for granted; they become nature, and their underlying assumptions recede into dogma and orthodoxy.
>
> The exile knows that in a secular and contingent world, homes are always provisional. Borders and barriers, which enclose us within the safety of familiar territory, can also become prisons, and are often defended beyond reason or necessity. Exiles cross borders, break barriers of thought and experience. . . .
>
> Regard experiences as if they were about to disappear. What is it that anchors them in reality? What would

you save of them? What would you give up? Only someone who has achieved independence and detachment,
someone whose homeland is "sweet" but whose circumstances make it impossible to recapture that sweetness,
can answer those questions. (Such a person would also
find it impossible to derive satisfaction from substitutes
furnished by illusion or dogma.) . . .

Seeing the "entire world as a foreign land" makes
possible originality of vision. Most people are principally
aware of one culture, one setting, one home; exiles are
aware of at least two, and this plurality of vision gives
rise to an awareness of simultaneous dimensions, an
awareness that—to borrow a phrase from music—is
contrapuntal.

For an exile, habits of life, expression or activity in the
new environment inevitably occur against the memory
of these things in another environment.

Whether or not "exile" aptly describes a blind person is
not my concern; the term certainly *characterizes* a blind
person. The condition of banishment, a requisite for exile, is not usually the condition of blind persons in contemporary society. But the lived experience of the exile
has resonance for blind persons; it allows for the "contrapuntal" relationship between blindness and sightedness,
which is more fruitful to understanding than a sheer oppositional relationship. It allows for a counterpoint between blindness and sightedness where, unusual as it
might be, some version of harmony can be heard.

Blindness does "jerk" one out of one's homeland. The
usual assumptions about home, and the dogmatic language of seeing and sight, are no longer in play; sight loses
its orthodox stance. Life still resonates with the sound of

the homeland, but it is an echo. The natural connections between seeing and knowing, seeing and ability, seeing and accessibility, seeing and participation, fall away from the natural and social order as easily as they once adhered. For adventitiously blind persons, these connections are jerked asunder, and they must rely on their memory of the language and customs of the homeland to reestablish these connections. Congenitally blind persons must learn, for the first time and without benefit of memory, to make these connections in the absence of sight. Both must continually remind themselves that they do, after all, live in a "sighted world."

Blind persons remember the "homeland" of the visual world in the way that the exile remembers the sweetness of home. Since blindness expels one from the homeland of what Hegel (1967, 149–60) calls "sensual certainty" in the same way that the exile is banished from the homeland of "political certainty," one can experience sight only as a "sweet fragrance" in the midst of the "immediacy of reality" of blindness!

Regardless of the particular organization of a culture's ratio of senses, everyone in that culture is "at home" with the way their reality is sensually organized. This is what leads to sense-certainty and to the immediate reality of "what is." Only strangers to the culture experience the insecurity and uncertainty of an immediate reality shaped by a differently organized ratio of senses. In H. G. Wells's *Country of the Blind* (1927), the sighted character Nunez experiences this disjunction when he accidentally enters a valley populated only by blind persons. Though Nunez is insecure and uncertain about reality in relation to the citizens of the country, he is secure and certain in his understanding that sight, not blindness, provides "true" sense-certainty.

When a person becomes blind in her or his own culture, however, the situation is somewhat different. The sense-certainty of the homeland remains intact, but the blind person him- or herself is no longer "at home" there. Belonging to a homeland means participating in what Gadamer (1988, 19–28) calls the "*sensus communus.*" One way that blind persons can achieve this participation is to treat their sense-ratio, now reorganized by blindness, as "off" in relation to the certainty of sight. This does not make the blind person at home with sightedness, but it shows that the blind person at least knows where and what the homeland is. He or she may come to feel "at home" with this knowledge but will always be, to some degree, homeless in the land of sightedness. Being at home with blindness can only mean that one is reconciled to a "home away from home." The blind person must become reconciled to the fact that while one can hear, smell, and touch the homeland, seeing it will always be impossible.

In his discussion of the perception of "invisible objects," Merleau-Ponty (1964, 13) poses the problem, "How should we describe the existence of these absent objects or the non-visible parts of these present objects?" The "existence" of absent or invisible objects is not part of Merleau-Ponty's problem; that these objects exist is not in question. "Description" is the problem. Given the existence of a thing, how do we describe it without seeing it?

The problem raised by Merleau-Ponty's phenomenological philosophy is the same problem raised by blindness. The existence of the visible "homeland" is not in question even though it is invisible to blindness. The problem for blind persons is how to describe this non-visible homeland. The sighted person's description of absent objects begins with the phenomenological premise that these objects *could* be seen if they were present—if they were in the person's visual field. The blind person's description of these objects, in contrast, begins with the premise that they *should* be seen, present or not, if the person *had* a visual field.

The descriptions of sighted persons rest on an empirical imperative insofar as absent objects are seeable despite their absence. For blind persons, these descriptions rest on a moral imperative insofar as absent *and* present objects are seeable despite blindness. Objects *should* be seen. For blind persons, *all* objects are always-already present despite their always-already absence. The homeland of the "sighted world" is never absent insofar as it is experienced in the ubiquitous sense of "omnipresence."

Blind persons are at home with their blindness when they are reconciled to the understanding that their home (blindness) is an "anomaly" and a regrettable one at that. But they must also be able to describe the visible world from which they are estranged. They can, and do, describe things in terms of the way they feel and sound, but they must also use the language of the sighted world if they are to lay claim to legitimate citizenship and not be banished to a purely private world, a *sensus privatus*. This is why blind persons use words like "see" and "look," and "see you later," and why we participate in activities such as "watching television" and making "eye contact." In this way (among others) we are able to participate in the *sensus communus*. All of us move and live "between" the private and public realms. We have private homes in our public homeland and we live in and between these homes. But blind persons carry their private homes with them in a way that sighted people do not. The home of blindness cannot be left behind when a blind person enters the home of sightedness. Blind persons always run the risk of living in *sensus privatus*. But blind persons have a further problem: How does one describe oneself as one who lives in absence and knows it? How does a blind person describe her or himself as a sighted person with the sight missing? How do blind persons, forced to carry their homes of blindness with them, describe themselves as belonging in the homeland of the sighted world, in *sensus communus*? How do blind persons describe their need and desire for residence in two homes? How does a blind person live with "dual citizenship"?

These questions are not easily answered, but they are always present, animating the life of anyone who has a home away from home. They raise the problem of creating and sustaining the integrity of both these homes. Being "at home with blindness" is to be an anomaly in the sighted world, and thinking of oneself as an anomaly does little for a blind person's quest for integrity and dignity. In fact, such a self-description effectively strips one of integrity in relation to blindness, and certainly in relation to being "at home" with blindness. Anomalies, to this way of thinking, are accidental; things should have been otherwise. But for disease or accident, blind persons should and would be able to see. When we see blindness in this way we see it as a home unworthy of habitation. This leaves the blind person with only one choice—to be at home *with* blindness and not *in* blindness. It is to choose sightedness as the only worthy homeland. But the question becomes, "How can I be sighted without sight?"

However one answers this question, the question itself presupposes that blindness is an uninhabitable home. But that does not mean that the blind person can somehow magically escape the condition of blindness; to the contrary, the blind person must find a way to live with blindness, to overcome the inescapable physiological fact of blindness.

This was how I understood my blindness before I had Smokie—as a condition that I had to overcome—and I believed that Smokie would help me do so. But my understanding soon began to change.

AT HOME WITH SMOKIE

Smokie quickly became familiar with his new surroundings, a radius of approximately two miles from our house. It did not take him very long to get to know the rest of his new city, either. Judging from the speed and excitement with which he worked, Smokie seemed to enjoy exploring his new social and physical environment.

Smokie has always been very willing and eager to work. I need only say "Let's go, Smokie" or touch his harness and he comes running, wagging his tail. Despite his animal nature, Smokie seems very much at home in human society. The strictly human idea of guiding a blind person appears to come naturally to him. I found Smokie's eagerness contagious. I was soon just as eager to work with Smokie as he was to work with me, and our work became just as natural to me as it was to him. I was beginning to feel at home in our work together and, as surprising as it was to me, I was beginning to find a home in my blindness.

Tanya was surprised by this, too. Before Smokie, she was the primary bridge between me and sightedness. She often served as my guide to restaurants, movies, and shopping, but now she was being displaced by Smokie, and it took us some time to adjust to this. Because of Smokie's speed and because I needed to focus my attention on his movements, Tanya and I stopped our practice of walking together hand in hand, though she did still continue to guide. As we approached some obstacle on the street, Tanya would warn us, "You're coming up to a newspaper stand," or "You're going to have to go around that car." I no longer needed her guidance, but she still needed to guide me. Tanya and I both had to understand the difference Smokie was making to my blindness. He was now the bridge to sightedness and was leading me confidently "into my blindness." We realized that being "at home" with blindness was a standard which was quickly being replaced by being "in blindness." Tanya too was experiencing this change, and *my* blindness was becoming, more than ever before, *our* blindness. All of us had to come to terms with our new situation.

Despite the extensive interaction I have with Tanya and others, I experience a kind of aloneness with Smokie. We are together in a large city in the midst of a multitude of people, but we are together *alone*. Alone together, Smokie and I explore and experience the kaleidoscopic sensuality of a large city, and our close focus on each other transforms this kaleidoscope into a sensual order. A magical metamorphosis takes place, whereby every mundane step becomes a physical and social adventure.

Our aloneness begins with our need to concentrate. Smokie needs to attend to an endless stream of stimuli — vehicular and pedestrian traffic, curbs, obstacles of various kinds on the street, the location of buildings, direction, and so on. He needs to make sure there is enough space for clear passage for me as well as for him. All of this means that Smokie is constantly making judgments. At the same time, he is concentrating intently on me, on my voice commands and hand signals and on how best to carry them out. I, meanwhile, am concentrating on Smokie. I follow his every move as he gives it to me through his harness. Like him, I am concentrating on a vast array of stimuli. I attend to sounds, smells, and changes in air flow that often indicate that we have moved past a building and toward an intersection. Alone together, we concentrate. Where we go is my decision. How we get there is his.

Walking with another person is next to impossible when Smokie is guiding me. For one thing, we are simply too fast for people to walk with us. Then there is the focus that Smokie and I share together; it is impossible to carry on a conversation with someone while working with Smokie this closely. Walking with someone else distracts us from our work and from our experience of the world.

Smokie and I walk alone together "in blindness." Whether Smokie knows that I am blind in the way that I or other people know it, I cannot say. But he does know. I became convinced of this the first time he guided me without harness, leash, or collar. One night approximately two months after our arrival home, I took Smokie out for his final relief time. As we exited the front door I said

"backyard" to Smokie and we proceeded up the driveway that leads to the rear of our house. As I walked slowly
up the driveway that night, Smokie suddenly pushed me
with his body and then came to a stop directly in front of
me. I was surprised and puzzled. Reaching out in front of
me, I felt the trunk of a car that Smokie had stopped me
from walking into. On another occasion, the harness
broke as we were working down a busy street. Broken harness in my right hand and Smokie's leash in my left, I
said, "Smoke, you have to find us a streetcar. It's up to
you." Without any further commands, he did, and we
made our way home.

Tanya tells me that Smokie is constantly looking at me.
He will guide me with his body when he is out of harness. When we move through particularly narrow spaces,
Smokie turns his head and looks at me. Exactly what
Smokie knows and how he knows it will always remain a
mystery. My life with Smokie will always be shrouded in
the essential mystery of the human/nature relationship.

What is not mysterious but very clear is that Smokie
does not treat my blindness as a bother, nuisance, or inconvenience. He gives no indication that he cares about
any social conceptions of blindness; he is not concerned
with self-pity or the pity of others. Blindness does not
seem to be a particularly positive thing to him, either,
but simply an occasion for him to work, to be a decisive actor in a social world. *This* is what I have learned
from Smokie. My blindness is an occasion for me to act
decisively and to think about what is important. When
Smokie is working, he is making decisions, decisions
that I emphatically abide by. I too make decisions when
Smokie guides me, and he emphatically abides by them.
We operate decisively, alone together.

Smokie decides how we will get where we are going in the midst of human society. His judgment takes me and my blindness into account. *He* is not going anywhere; *we* are. He bases his judgment of the best way to a destination not on what is best for him or for me, but what is best for us. Smokie has also turned my blindness into an occasion for me. With Smokie, I see a world which has never been seen by a sighted person. Alone together, Smokie and I decide what is best for us in a sighted human world, a world with which we are familiar but from which we are estranged.

In her essay on "Understanding," Arendt (1994, 308) says, "[Understanding] is the specifically human way of being alive; for every single person needs to be reconciled to a world into which he was born a stranger and in which, to the extent of his distinct uniqueness, he always remains a stranger." Understanding begins with the realization of our uniqueness as it relates to the world into which we are born. Through this dialectic we begin to imagine a self, as that self is formed through social interaction with the world. The self develops a familiarity with the world while sustaining its uniqueness—thus its estrangement from the world. In Mead's terms (1934), the "I" is not destroyed through the formation of a "we." Instead, the two co-exist in the social world expressed in the interminable dialectic of estrangement and familiarity. We become "reconciled" to the world, but we will always be to some degree estranged from it as well, "to the extent of [our] distinct uniqueness."

Blindness is one defining feature of my uniqueness. Blindness is not simply the negation of sight: It is a way of sensing the world and a way of being in the world that is influenced by such social conditions as place and time of birth, age of onset of blindness, social class, gender, race, and all the individual particularities that each of us has. Our uniqueness influences our understanding of blindness as much as our membership in society does. To recall Said's metaphor, the uniqueness of blindness itself springs from its contrapuntal relation to sightedness.

Like Said's exile, the blind person knows that in a world of contingency, homes are provisional. We can be sighted today and blind tomorrow. Like the exile's experience of crossing political and geographical boundaries, crossing the border from sightedness to blindness provides for the possibility of breaking the barriers of "thought and experience." Unlike sighted persons, blind persons are not imprisoned by the view that eyesight provides the *only* way of seeing and knowing. When we are able to see blindness not merely as the absence of sight but as another legitimate way of being in the world, we have an opportunity to cross a barrier of thought and experience. We grasp the truth that the sighted world is only one possible "homeland," and we reconcile ourselves to the provisional nature of that homeland.

If we follow Said and "regard experiences as if they were about to disappear," the concept of blindness as a distinct homeland gains depth. Visual experience has disappeared for blind persons, and we regard experiences as if they were about to appear. The estrangement brought to life by blindness raises the question of what anchors reality. Said says that only someone who has lost their native homeland, someone who has achieved "independence and detachment," can answer the question of what is worth preserving in experience.

But the achievement of this independence and detachment means that a blind person must reconcile him- or
herself to the unique estrangement it offers in relation to
the homeland of sightedness. The blind person knows
that the homeland of sightedness is "sweet," but blindness does not permit the recapturing of this sweetness.
The sweetness of sight is given up in order to "save" the
conception of reality as anchored in the ability to see.
The conception that blindness is a mere "handicap" to
experiencing reality is an "illusion" to one who understands her or his blindness as a way of "seeing." When
sightedness is seen as the "paramount reality" (Schutz),
the result is a "handicapped" rather than a blind person.
Blind persons save sightedness as that which anchors reality as the "sweetness of familiarity" with the homeland
of sightedness. This allows us to imagine sightedness and,
moreover, to take the point of view of sighted others. Seeing sightedness as *the* anchor of reality, however, leads
one to conceive of blindness as a "handicap" to knowing
and participating in the "reality of the sighted world."
But this does not provide for any understanding of the
essential difference between being blind and being
sighted. It provides only for the humanistic understanding that "I am a person who happens to be blind."

This expression is the dogma produced by the illusion
that the only homeland is contained within the borders
of sight. The only blind person who derives satisfaction
from the substitutes of illusion and dogma is one who has
not reconciled their essential estrangement and essential
familiarity, one who does not imagine understanding as
a life lived between birth and death. This type of understanding provides for the possibility of a "blind person"
as distinct from the humanistic version of blindness as

one who "happens to be blind." The latter understands him- or herself as a person steeped only in the familiarity of the sighted world, while the former is reconciled to an "estranged familiarity."

In Said's terms, original vision is the ability to see the entire world as a foreign land. "Most people are principally aware of only one culture, one setting, one home; exiles are aware of at least two." Blindness provides an opportunity for this kind of "original vision," because it contains the awareness that sightedness is only one of many possible "cultures." Sightedness is socially achieved through language, gestures, customs, and the rest of the paraphernalia of a culture. This "vision" allows blind persons explicitly to achieve familiarity with sighted culture by reproducing its language and folkways.

Persons who "happen to be blind" are similar to sighted persons insofar as they do not engage in the achievement of sightedness as a cultural production or even as imitation. There is no irony. Blind persons, on the other hand, possess the vision to see not only their production of sightedness but also that of sighted others. This original vision allows blindness and sightedness to be seen not as mere opposites but as two contrapuntal ways of being in the world. The irony and harmony of this vision exists in this: Regardless of what it sees, sight cannot see itself (Merleau-Ponty, 1962). Regardless of what it cannot see, blindness can see sight as essentially requiring social and cultural achievement. Thus strangeness and familiarity become ironically harmonized in their reformation as "estranged familiarity." Following Said, there is a "plurality of vision" possible for the exile, in this case the blind person, which is not available to the sighted person. In this plurality of vision, or contrapuntal "awareness of simultaneous dimensions," lies the pleasure of blindness.

This is the sort of pleasure I derive from my life and work with Smokie. We are an "odd couple" as we move through the world—a man and a dog moving as one, alone together. We move through the world figuring it out together. We depend on one another and are largely independent of sighted others. No sighted person moves through the world in the way Smokie and I do; no sighted person understands it the way we do. Smokie and I are at once familiar with the world and estranged from it.

I am estranged from the social world because, unlike most people, I am blind. Smokie is estranged because he is a dog. That most people want neither to be blind nor to be dogs is what Smokie and I have in common. My estrangement stems from living and working in the human world as a blind person, while Smokie's stems from his living and working in the human world as a dog. We represent the contrapuntal relation between blindness and sightedness and between society and nature.

Despite the fact that Smokie is a dog, I often get the sense that he is more easily accepted by society than I am. Smokie's presence in society represents "domesticated nature." If we believe the evolutionists, there was a time in our distant past when people began to see the wild wolf as potentially useful, and this marked the genesis of the domesticated dog. People sought out only those wolves that exhibited traits conducive to taming and human control. Over time and slowly, as evolutionists see it, only those animals that proved useful and were able to adapt their wild ways to the ways of people—those who became "well-behaved citizens"—remained in human society. Their offspring inherited these traits and "natural selection" was on its way to evolving the "domesticated dog."

Today dogs are as much a part of North American life as people are. A glance at any book on dog breeds will reveal explanations of the original use of the dog and the uses for which it was bred. Dogs are almost universally seen as useful, as loyal companions, as therapeutic— in short, as "man's best friend." The once foreign land of human society is now *domos* to the dog—the dog is at home in human society. Like any foreigner, the dog has become a product of "naturalization." Naturalized though it may be, however, the dog is still a part of nature in a way that human beings are not. At home as the dog is in human society, the dog still maintains the separate *domos* of its nature.

Unlike the dog, blind persons are not understood by contemporary society as products of domestication. Society does not typically see blindness as a useful trait. To this day, blind persons still must argue their own usefulness and must convince others that, despite their blindness, they are still able to do useful things.

Even though blindness has recently been transformed from an "inability" into a "disability,"[2] it has not become something valued or desired by society. Blind persons are at home in society insofar as they *become* blind *in* society. Blindness is not viewed as a condition produced by the workings of human society, so society takes no responsibility for the appearance of blindness.[3] Blindness is not like poverty, unemployment, racism, sexism, or other "social problems," which are typically conceived as potentially remediable if only people could rid themselves of prejudice. Blindness is seen as a physical condition; its only "social" dimension is its amenity to rehabilitation.

Thus Smokie and I live and work alone together in our society, he as domesticated nature and I as an example of nature "gone wrong." Smokie is a reminder of society's power over nature, while I remind society of nature's power over it. We are at home in our society and are familiar with its landscape and customs, though Smokie's familiarity comes from the point of view of his domesticated nature and mine comes from the point of view of blindness. We remain foreigners in our homeland despite our familiarity with it. We see our homeland from the point of view of "estranged familiarity."

Smokie and I live and work in a state of "unnaturalness." It is as unnatural for Smokie to guide as it is for me not to see. Alone together as we are in our unnaturalness, it seems natural to be together. I did not have a sense of this "naturalness" before I had Smokie; my blindness always seemed unnatural to me. But from the beginning Smokie appeared to me to undertake his unnatural guide work very naturally, and he expected the same from me. He expected me both to follow and to lead him, and he expected me to expect the same from him. I soon began to feel at home with this unnatural state of affairs. Smokie made a place for my blindness in his life and I made a place for him in mine. We are at home in our estrangement and at home in our familiarity with sighted human society. Smokie and I have a unique appearance in the world which gives us a unique "look" at it. We are dependent on our familiarity with sighted society and yet maintain an independence from it through our estrangement. I want now to look more closely at the idea of independence.

THE SEARCH FOR A GUIDE AS A SEARCH FOR INDEPENDENCE

The goal of independence for blind persons suggests first and foremost the need for a guide, conventionally understood as "another pair of eyes." The search for this guide takes relatively little time and energy. Blind persons need only look to those who can see; this is "only natural." Reliance on a sighted guide is not natural in the way that the gift of vision itself is, of course; it is reliance on a person who, although naturally endowed with vision, is immersed in a social order. Both blind person and sighted guide are committed to a social and cultural order. This form of guide presents no challenge to the social order as it is conventionally understood. It amounts to the social order leading the social order.

Other concerns in relation to the sighted guide center on social conceptions of blindness, as we have seen. Blind persons who rely on sighted others are typically seen, and sometimes see themselves, as "dependent." Even though sighted persons can be proficient guides, and can perform other daily tasks for blind persons such as feeding and dressing them, these guides are understood as the source of dependence. The interpretation at work is that the sighted guide transforms the blind person into the one who is dependent. Even when a blind person is able to accomplish everyday tasks, relying on a sighted guide only in exceptional circumstances, the stigma of dependence remains. Using a sighted guide is not seen as a way for a blind person to conduct her life independently.

An orientation and mobility instructor for blind persons described one of his clients to me in this way.

> He takes a taxi everywhere. No matter where he goes, he takes a taxi. This is just not independent mobility. My first job is to somehow teach him that he needs to strive for independence.

Obviously, this blind person was getting wherever he wanted to go, but the instructor did not see this man as "independently" mobile. As proficient as he was in the use of taxis, he was regarded as dependent.

The instructor continued:

> He's actually doing not too bad with the long cane. We've only had about a half dozen lessons. It'll just take a little while for him to get confident. But as soon as he gets that confidence, he'll travel independently with his cane and he won't have to rely on taxis any more.

Taxis and long canes both provide the possibility of mobility, but the instructor sees them as having unequal status. The question is: *On what* is the taxi-user dependent and *from what* is the man with the cane independent? On one level, the answer is clear: Using taxis makes blind persons dependent on sighted others for mobility, whereas the long cane makes it possible for them to get around on their own and for this reason is preferred regardless of efficiency. The instructor's distinction between the taxi and the cane suggests that questions of dependence and independence are embedded in a more complicated web of social relations than the issue of mere efficiency can explain.

I questioned the instructor as to his preference for the cane.

> *RM:* Just humor me. I just want to get this clear. Suppose I said that taxis are safer and more efficient than the white cane. You know, if you're rich enough, why not just take taxis wherever you want to go? I mean, a blind person can even hire a sighted person. This gets the job done too. How would you respond to this?
>
> *Instructor:* Well, you're right except for one thing. The blind person wouldn't be independent. He would be relying strictly on sighted persons. He wouldn't be doing anything for himself. This is important for all of us, not just blind people. We should all do things for ourselves. Blind persons are no different. If you just take cabs or just use sighted guides, you're just relying on other people. It might be good for a while but sooner or later . . . you know, you lose your self-esteem. You lose that sense of accomplishment. Then, you never know anything. People just take you here and there but you never know how you got there. You don't know anything about the world around you. The long cane, well that's different. That means you get to know that world. If everything else is okay, you'll rely on your other senses, you know, hearing, smell, you know. The long cane is not like a sighted person. It's part of you. It's an extension of your hand, your finger really. You then get oriented to your environment. That's why it's called orientation and mobility. You get to know the world, by yourself. You don't have to rely on anyone else. Oh sure, once in a while you can use a sighted guide. You know,

if you're going to a café with a friend, and you're going the same way, well sure, take an elbow. But that's just convenience. In yourself, you know you could get there without the sighted guide. That's the difference, that's the important thing. You've got your other senses, and your cane. Those things let you see without your eyesight, if you know what I mean? You do things on your own, you're independent and you feel good.

Along the same lines, a blind university student said this:

Crowd control, that's what I call my stick. When I go down the street, people get out of my way in a hurry. Then sometimes I go from side to side on the sidewalk. You know, some sighties probably think I'm drunk. But I'm just looking around. I like to see what's around . . . once in a while I'll grab an arm but I don't like to do that. You know, I do it for them sighties. Makes them feel good. But I can get along just fine on my own. Actually it's better on my own. That way I know exactly where I am. You can't trust them sighties. You know, sometimes they take you where you don't want to go. Then they never let you know anything. I trust my crowd control.

We can begin to see that a blind person's search for a guide is not motivated simply by practical or technical considerations. Practicality alone would lead such a search directly to sighted others, but this is not the preferred destination. The search for a guide is a search for a way to move through the world with freedom, and for a way to come to know the world in the process. The cane allows this kind of freedom. Unlike a taxi or other sighted guide, it becomes an extension of the body, a part of one's self, and therefore represents self-reliance and independence.

Reliance on sighted others does not permit such freedom and knowledge, which can only be attained when blind persons are independent of sighted others. This is the typical understanding of independence. That blind persons can do things for themselves presupposes another kind of independence—the independence to make decisions about the things they do. Blind persons are not dependent on sighted persons for these decisions; independence, therefore, is understood as independence *from* sighted persons.

This conception of independence evokes the idea of self-reliance. It is the *self* that blind persons rely on as a way to move through the world. To satisfy the sense of self-reliance, the long cane is conceived as not only a guide but also as an essential part of the blind person and is often given a name, e.g., "crowd control." The inanimate cane is given life when it is endowed with the status of part of the human body and is thus transformed into a "natural endowment." As such, the cane represents the *self* and therefore independence. The cane permits blind persons to interpret *themselves* as guiding themselves through the world. This is independent guiding. But it is an independence from more than merely sighted persons.

Independent mobility means that blind persons can develop the ability to move through the world independent of sight and independent of other selves. The blind person, in becoming self reliant, transforms him- or herself from one "without sight" into a "blind self." This blind person can now "look around," can "see" the world, can know it and move through it. This conception of independence conceives of blindness as a condition which can be adjusted to and coped with and does not have to lead to dependence. This "blind self" understands that it is capable of knowing and moving through the "sighted world" and can be just as efficient at doing so as sighted people are. This understanding of independence conceives of the difference between blind persons and sighted persons as a difference in technique. The world remains "sighted" and persons remain either blind or sighted. Blind selves are thus transformed into persons *who happen to be blind.*

This interpretive framework suggests that there is nothing essential about blindness. It is merely the condition of "missing-sight." But sight can be replaced by making better use of the remaining senses and by finding a guide that can become part of the person. Nothing essential, according to this view, is transformed by blindness. The blind person is merely a sighted person who is missing his sight. For example, here is what a blind lawyer had to say about his blindness:

> I don't think of myself as disabled. I'm like everyone else. I just happen to be blind. Blindness is no big deal. All it is is a nuisance and an inconvenience. Like any other nuisance, it can easily be overcome. There's lots of technology around, especially nowadays. There is no excuse for any blind person not to live a normal life.

Blindness "gets in the way" of living a normal life, but technology can solve the problem. It can remove the nuisance and open the way to normalcy. Since everyone's life is fraught with nuisance and inconvenience, blind persons are no different from anyone else and insofar as everyone must cope with nuisance, there is no excuse for blind persons not to do so.

Still, blind persons *must* search for a guide. Even though a guide, like the long cane, may replace sight, it simultaneously brings blindness to the fore. Guides do more than guide. Whatever form they take, guides are a product of the social and cultural order. As such, they *symbolize* that order.[4] We see *meaning* when we see blindness. We see tragedy, courage, self-pity, determination, helplessness, a sixth sense, mystery, and sometimes even nuisance and inconvenience. Guides guide blind persons through the world and guide others to the meaning of blindness, which otherwise remains trapped in the collective consciousness. The search for a guide is inevitably a search not only for independence but also for the meaning of blindness.

INDEPENDENCE AND INCOMPLETENESS

Independence always means independence *from* something. But being independent from something also means being dependent on something else. I am no longer dependent on the white cane or sighted guides, but I am dependent on Smokie to get around. Independence really means "dependence on the right thing(s)" and is thus essentially a moral issue.

Children are raised in our culture with the aim of making them independent members of society. The independent scholar is the aim of graduate school training; financial independence is the aim of a paying job. All of these things aim at independence by providing something that is missing and without which the person in question is considered incomplete. Blindness releases the ideas of incompleteness and independence in the same way that the dog guide releases the idea of blindness. Despite collective representations to the contrary, blindness is not merely an isolated physiological condition, but a "gestalt," a realm of activity which in our society is framed primarily by the disciplines of ophthalmology and rehabilitation. Even though these disciplines typically understand themselves as acting on blindness and thus as independent of it, their action serves to achieve an individual and collective sense of what blindness is, and they are thus deeply implicated in the social meaning of blindness.

Ophthalmologists view blindness as an abnormal physiology, and medical treatment is its first approach to this "abnormality." If blindness does not respond to medical treatment, then it must be addressed through rehabilitation. Counselling, Braille, orientation and mobility training, and technologies such as talking computers become the means to independence. The aim of rehabilitation is for blind persons to develop the ability to conduct the activities of everyday life by themselves, independent of sighted others. By becoming dependent on techniques provided by rehabilitation, the theory goes, blind persons can become independent of the "incompleteness" caused by an "abnormal physiology."

The concept that blindness may *itself* be an essential occasion for independence and decisive action is foreign to the theories of ophthalmology and rehabilitation. These disciplines are efficient at developing and providing "coping technologies," but they tend to leave the blind person's need for integrity *as* a blind person out of the picture. They see blindness as a purely negative condition and, more importantly, as a condition external to self that must somehow be gotten around. There is no question that blind persons must learn how to do things by and for themselves, but *how* they do so, and how they construe their identity as blind persons, are questions that ophthalmology and rehabilitation cannot fully address.

GRACEFUL INDEPENDENCE

I have already shown how achieving mobility with Smokie was a decisive act on my part that involved emotion as well as reasoned thought about the place of blindness and sightedness in my life. Dog guides can be seen as more or less efficient "mobility devices" in relation to the long cane. Efficiency, however, is only a small part of the ability to "get around"; it does not take into account that the dog guide can also teach a blind person many things. Smokie is much more to me than an effective mobility device. We do get from here to there effectively. My dependence on him has given me a sense of independence from sighted others. But more than this, Smokie has given me my blindness. He has taught me that I am *not* a person who happens to be blind. Smokie has given me the opportunity to become a "blind person"—a decisive actor.

My relationship with Smokie is imbued with grace; he graciously gives me independence and I graciously accept it from him—it is a "graceful independence" that begins with the way we move together. When Eustis saw the blind man moving toward her, dog firmly in hand, she saw confidence and assurance. With Smokie firmly in hand, I experience the same confidence and assurance that Smokie knows what he is doing. I know that I am safe with the same taken-for-granted certainty that others experience through the sense of sight.

More than this, we move as one. A pedestrian who witnessed us crossing an intersection remarked, "You two look like you're choreographed." When I want to cross a street at an intersection and then to cross the intersecting street, we begin by crossing the first street, until Smokie stops at the up-curb. I ask him to stay and then give him the command "forward." After two steps, I again ask him to stay. Moving my right foot and arm to the right, I say "right." Then, again, "stay." I then ask him to go forward and he stops at the down-curb, ready to cross the second street. Complicated as these movements are, we perform them quickly and in the midst of busy pedestrian traffic. Crossing a busy intersection is complicated and can be dangerous for a blind person, but Smokie makes it look easy and well-choreographed —in a word, graceful.

Smokie and I move in and out of pedestrian traffic in the same graceful, well-choreographed way. Everything Smokie does comes to me through the harness. I feel each of his steps and I step with him. I feel every variation of speed, every change of direction, the most subtle variation in the path Smokie is taking, and I feel myself moving with the subtle smoothness and grace that Smokie gives me through the harness. With him, I can start, stop, and "turn on a dime." He often has to stop suddenly or turn quickly to avoid a carelessly moving pedestrian, a cyclist, or even an automobile, and he has prevented injury on many occasions.

Smokie has returned my body to me. Even though I could walk quickly in my "10 percent days," I did not take the joy in walking that I do now, and I never walked with the grace that Smokie has given me. Moving with Smokie invariably conjures up my days as an athlete on the football field. I followed my blockers with the same precision with which I now follow Smokie. Running through a field of defenders, I looked for any semblance of an opening and moved through it twisting, turning, stopping, and starting. In the open field, I ran as quickly as I could, changing directions as quickly and as often as necessary to avoid being tackled. Smokie has returned me to my athletic days, when I was "at one" and "in tune" with my body. The body movements that came naturally to me on the football field are once again natural. I rarely use the term "working dog" to describe Smokie, but I do call him an athlete.

The independence I get from Smokie includes this natural movement of my body, a movement I now have independent of sight. The grace with which I move with Smokie has given me an independence that has very little to do with independence as it is conventionally understood in relation to blindness. Smokie has given me movement "in blindness." The goal of any blind person is to live and move and work in a world even though that world is visually absent. Yet independence is more than that, for blindness is not merely the absence of the visual; it is also a presence. Blindness is an occasion to *make* the visual present through means other than sight. The senses of touch, smell, and hearing can bring one into touch with the never-ending movement of the visual. This is what I mean by the "grace of independence." Smokie has given me a glimpse of my homeland from the point of view of my home-in-blindness. I am "in home" with my blindness and, with Smokie's help, I carry this home gracefully through the homeland of sightedness. Blindness is now essential and no longer happenstance.

In order to learn from blindness, its "grace of teaching" must be revitalized. This is the most important path to which Smokie guided me. With his guidance, I embarked on the path of revitalizing my blindness as a teacher. Smokie guided me to the understanding that I would be on this path forever and that he and I, in our travels, continuously embark on the adventure of lifelong learning. In my adventures with Smokie, I have learned much about my society. Because we are an "odd couple," Smokie and I provoke the interest and curiosity of people, and we become involved in a continuous flow of interaction with others as we travel through our world. Such interaction is inevitably influenced by preconceptions about blindness and dog guides; our reputation precedes us in our travels. I want now to address this reputation and its relation to our identity, both individually and together.

CHAPTER FIVE

The Power of Reputation

"He sure is a smart dog. Is it a he?"
"Yeah."
"Well, he's sure smart."
"Yeah, he sure is."

MUCH OF THE interaction Smokie and I experience centers on his reputation as a dog guide and on mine as a blind person. As we move through our social world, people feel compelled to talk to us or about us, and their comments reveal their understanding of these identities. The concepts of reputation and identity are connected, especially in their interactional expression. As Mead (1934) and Cooley (1909) have shown, who and what we are is influenced by how others conceive of us. We interact with one another through the mediation of these conceptions, and the "selves" that we form in turn influence the conceptions others have of us.

The "generalized other" with which Smokie and I interact is the "human sighted world"; it is the "looking glass" we face. My essential other is the social world understood as "see-able" and populated by others who can see. For Smokie, the essential other is a society populated by human beings with particular conceptions of, and relations to, nature. This is the world in which Smokie and I are immersed—a world in which I am "no longer" sighted and he is "not yet" human (Arendt 1956, 9). The world through which Smokie and I move is neither fully sighted, fully human, nor fully natural. We move "between" these ontologies in the "no longer and not yet."[1]

INTELLIGENT AND WELL TRAINED

"What a smart dog!"

"Man, really well-trained dog!"

"See, that doggy is helping him. He's blind. The doggy helps him walk around."

"Oh, no, don't touch that dog. He's a working dog. He's working for that man. That man is blind."

"Wow, look at that dog! That's excellent!"

"Oh, a dog, I didn't even see him! He sure is well trained!"

Smokie and I hear these comments and others like them whenever we are in public places—waiting at a traffic light, passing someone on a street, sitting on a subway or in a café.[2] Most people speak about rather than directly to us, and always in a voice loud enough for us to hear.

Comments about Smokie's behavior are often complimentary. I never ask whether someone thinks Smokie is smart or well-trained, but people offer their opinions freely when they see him in harness. The presence of a dog guide team is, apparently, reason enough for comment. People often compliment Smokie's intelligence without benefit of any direct evidence. Thus, a stranger on the subway:

"He sure is a smart dog. Is it a he?"
"Yeah."
"Well, he's sure smart."
"Yeah, he sure is."

I was sitting at the time, while Smokie lay on the floor beside me. This man told me that he had entered the subway at the last stop; he had seen Smokie do nothing but lie on the floor. Another conversation took place while Smokie and I were waiting for a friend in front of a bookstore.

"Boy, your dog is well-trained and smart."
"Thanks."
"How long does it take to train him like that?"
"He trained for about eight months or so."
"That's some smart dog."

Again, the person was a stranger who happened to be walking by. I was standing and Smokie was sitting at my side. Since we had been waiting for almost ten minutes, this person had had no opportunity to see Smokie do anything but sit.

It is certainly possible that a dog lying quietly on a

subway or sitting patiently in front of a bookstore can be interpreted as intelligent. People tend to see a well-behaved dog this way, especially when they think of dogs as naturally inclined to run and play. A dog sitting patiently in a public place may be seen as intelligent insofar as the dog is behaving contrary to natural inclinations. Perhaps such reasoning does, in part, account for unsolicited comments about Smokie's intelligence, but I suspect that Smokie's harness must have even more to do with it.

The harness symbolizes blindness and work; it means that Smokie is a working dog and that his work involves guiding a blind person. Without any direct evidence of his intelligence, these comments are as symbolic as Smokie's harness. They symbolically represent that a dog in harness, even when lying down, must be intelligent and well-trained. More than anything else, what tells people that Smokie is smart is the "reputation" of a dog in harness. They do not have to see Smokie actively at work, or to know anything about him in particular, only that he is in harness. The harness carries with it the reputation of dog guide and the characteristics that dog guides are reputed to possess, namely intelligence and a high level of training. These attributes, real as they might be, are especially noticeable and worthy of comment insofar as they reveal the assumption that the dog in harness is able to act contrary to natural inclinations. The dog must be well-trained to ignore "what comes naturally." Training teaches the dog to *control* her or his nature. The desire or need for such control, for training, certainly does come from the dog. Left to their own devices, dogs will behave *naturally* and will thus follow their natural inclinations. They will be controlled by nature. This is one more aspect of Smokie's identity that generates comments on his intelligence. Despite his harness, Smokie evokes the reputation of a dog—of any *natural* dog. But since he does not behave naturally, like any dog, Smokie is worthy and deserving of compliments.

Comments about Smokie's intelligence speak to his identity both as a dog with natural inclinations and as a working dog who has been trained to overcome his nature.[3] At the same time, however, that his training is assumed to explain this "overcoming," Smokie's nature is evoked as a way to account for his high level of training. Smokie is well-trained and has therefore overcome his nature. Smokie is well-trained, and is therefore *naturally* intelligent. Smokie's reputation begins and ends with concepts of nature. Indeed, it is the fact that he is an animal, and thus a representative of nature, that makes possible the compliments of strangers. Still, even though Smokie is interpreted within the membership category "dog," he is also interpreted as a particular dog. The category "dog" provides for the possibility of both "good" and "bad" dogs.

A similar sort of interpretive scheme is at work when children are complimented for good behavior or manners. Since these things do not come naturally to young children, they are praised for learning to share with others or for waiting their turn or for any of the other countless ways that they show they are becoming socialized. Likewise, adults usually greet a child's first step or first word with enthusiasm[4] First steps and first words are interpreted in the context of the child's body, or nature. A first step means that the child's body, its muscular development and coordination, is not yet fully developed. In the case of the first word, the child has not yet developed a full set of teeth or the ability to manipulate the tongue. The child is not yet fully socialized in the areas of walking, talking, or appropriate behavior and manners. In this sense, the child is closer to nature than to society. As the child begins to conform to social norms, adults praise and reward him or her. If a child walked or talked at any early age, she is a "quick learner." The child learns how to "behave," how to sit quietly, for example, even though she would rather run and play. Like the dog, the child is complimented on her ability to overcome natural inclinations. And, as in the case of the dog, compliments may come from strangers and may not necessarily be addressed to the child or parent.

Such compliments suggest the admiration human society feels for the overcoming of nature, interpreted as a powerful force that stands in opposition to society. Smokie in harness is an occasion for "seeing" nature's power being overcome and is thus as an occasion for praise. Smokie is complimented for behaving *so* "unnaturally" despite the fact that he is *so* "natural." His harness gives him the reputation of one who, while embodying nature, has conquered it. The harness makes Smokie "look like" a smart dog. *Some* dogs have the ability to overcome their nature[5] and thus *some* of them are intelligent.

THE WELL-BRED IDENTITY

Remarks about Smokie's intelligence spring from his identity as a dog guide. An equally important part of his identity as a working dog is his particular breed, and people tend to endow him with the traits they associate with Labrador Retrievers.

"He's a Lab, isn't he?"
"Yeah."
"They're great dogs!"
"They sure are."

Or:

"Boy, he's smart!"
"He is."
"Well, that's a Lab for you."

Another example:

"I hear they're using mostly Labs for seeing eye work now."
"Actually, some different breeds too."
"But, Labs are the best."
"He's one, so I agree."
"Yeah, they're the best suited."

Some people also remark on Smokie's color, and their comments always strike me as humorous. I find it difficult not to respond in kind.

"Is he a black lab?"
"No he's yellow."

"Oh, he's a black lab."
"Really! Thanks, I thought he was yellow."

After exchanges like these, I have to conceal my laughter as Smokie and I proceed down the street.
    Among the people who have commented on Smokie's

Labrador breed, one told me that he had a pet Lab, but I have never been approached by someone involved in dog training. Comments about Smokie's breed are not restricted to people on the street, either. A trainer at the school where Smokie was trained said,

> We use mostly Labs. Occasionally, we use crosses between Labs and Poodles, you know, for those blind people allergic to dogs. Kinda like "Labradoodles." They seem to work out okay. But no shepherds. The public seems to be afraid of German shepherds. They have a reputation for being aggressive. We used to use them, but we don't use them anymore. They're not as focused as Labs. They're distracted pretty easily. So we don't use them anymore.

Breed is one interpretive category used to account for the necessary qualities of a dog guide as opposed to the more general interpretive category of the species, dog. Both categories, however, allude to the nature of the dog. Whether a dog is a guide or a pet, it is assumed to possess the traits common to its breed. The notion of "breed" may be understood as a method for defining and fleshing out a dog's reputation.

Thus, any German shepherd may be seen as potentially aggressive. The dog guide trainer added, "Shepherds are too protective and then sometimes they get aggressive." Over-protectiveness, aggression, and lack of focus are not qualities conducive to dog guide work, and the public does not see such qualities as part of a dog guide's reputation. Focus and non-aggression, in contrast, are qualities that suit the Labrador Retriever to guide work. Dog guides in general, and Labs in particular, are reputed to possess such qualities.

The dog's reputation is couched in terms of the inherent nature of the breed as well as the inherent nature of the species. The dog's breed defines the particular traits that act to distinguish it from other breeds. In the same way, people are human and thus possess qualities and features particular to their species—*Homo sapiens.* But the analogy ends there. To attribute particular qualities to a person based on race, ethnicity, or even gender, is seen by contemporary Western society as racist or sexist stereotyping. Judgments about dog breeds are not typically seen as stereotyping (though this can happen, as when the owner of a Pit Bull, or a German shepherd for that matter, protests that his dog has been given a "bad rep"). Usually, however, dogs have "reputations" that are widely understood to come from their breed—they are ill-tempered or good-tempered, intelligent or stupid, aggressive or gentle. The identity politics debate[6] is a strictly human phenomenon that takes place outside the realm of nature. So far as I know, no one has yet been accused of "breedism" when speaking ill of a Black Lab or a German shepherd. We expect dogs to live up to their reputation and to express their identity. Commenting on a dog's behavior in relation to its breed is understood within the paradigm of identity/reputation, whereas commenting on a person's behavior in terms of ethnicity is understood within the paradigm of stereotyping. Thus "language use" does not distinguish humanity from nature. Instead "language is used" to *make* that distinction.

This is not to say that humans are not interpreted

within the paradigm of nature, since we often are. We are said to have a "biology" and to be part of the "animal kingdom"; we are sometimes described as the "human animal."[7] Even so, the idea that human beings are fundamentally different from and superior to animals points to the high value we place on the process of socialization—on becoming human—as well as on "individuality" as an ontology generated and sustained through the dialectic of the "individual and society." Natural as we are, our natures are inexorably bound to nurture.

Human beings, by this reasoning, are tied to nature but not determined by it. Dogs, on the other hand, are understood *as* nature, and as such they require training. As human beings, we understand the concept of training within the humanistic categories of education and socialization.[8] This is why we are often amazed by the abilities of a dog guide, even by its ability to distinguish left from right, when we are not amazed at the same ability in a person. This is also why it is not stereotyping when we speak of a dog's reputation in terms of its breed, but why it is stereotyping when we speak of a person's reputation in terms of race or ethnicity.

Dog guide trainers consistently make use of the dog's identity as nature, and of the particular traits of its breed, when instructing blind persons in the use and care of their dog guides. In the words of one trainer,

> Remember, your dog is still just a dog. You have to give him time to be that. Not just relieving him and feeding him, that's obvious. You have to let him be a dog once in a while. Actually, you should let him be that every day. He needs play time. Your dog has to have a chance just to be a dog, just to play.

Presumably it is easy for blind persons to forget that their dog guide is "just a dog." The dog guide can do so much: guide people around obstacles, take them safely across streets, find chairs, escalators, telephones, sit quietly in a restaurant while the handler is having dinner, and much more. Given all of this, it is easy to forget that the dog guide is "just a dog" that also needs to play.

But what is forgotten when we forget this, and what do we have to remember? For most of his day, Smokie does many of the things that people do. He lines up in banks, finds the counter at stores, spends time in bars, restaurants, and other public places, watches out for traffic, and all the rest. He watches out for me. Being so "person-like" in so many ways, he makes it easy for me to forget that he is not a person. Most of the time, Smokie acts as if he *were* human—he does the things that humans do and does them responsibly. I must be mindful that Smokie is "just a dog." I must be mindful of Smokie as nature and of my attachment to nature. I must remember to allow Smokie to be who he is, to be nature, to play, to pee, to sniff.

THE IRONY OF PERSONALITY

While the identity and reputation of a dog guide are understood within the general interpretive categories dog as nature, dog as species, and dog as breed, more particular categories also come into play. Ironically, one such category is "personality." Somewhere in this web of nature, breed, and training lurks the feature of personality. Behind the idea of "just a dog" exists a particular, individual personality—a dog like no other dog.

Within the arena of dog guide work, the notion of

personality expresses itself in several ways. For one thing, it must be determined whether a particular dog, its nature and breed notwithstanding, is suited for dog guide work. This decision[9] is not, however, separable from the idea of nature. The dog's particular breeding, its individual blood line as opposed to its general breed, is taken into account. Thus genetic predisposition becomes an important factor in determining whether or not a dog possesses the potential for dog guide work.[10] Many dog guide schools have their own breeding program, in which dogs are bred for the express purpose of dog guide work. Some schools enhance their own program by acquiring dogs bred outside the school. In both cases, the dog's personal genetic make-up is taken into account.

One of the information sessions held at the school I attended focused on blood lines. Two trainers informed us of the blood lines of our particular dogs. This is what they had to say about Smokie's blood line:

> Smokie's father was American. His mom was Canadian. The stud sired many dog guides. The brood bitch, Smokie's mom, had two litters. Smokie was in the second. There were fifteen in total. Six of them are working dog guides now. Then there is Smokie and three more are being trained. He comes from good stock, he's got a good blood line. His dad sired about four generations of dog guides.

In addition to being, first, a dog, and, second, a Black Lab, Smokie was considered a good candidate for guide work because of his individual genes. Since there were many dog guides in Smokie's family, he was thought to be genetically predisposed to such work. That Smokie's parents produced several dog guides was not treated as an accident or coincidence by the staff, but as an indication that Smokie would probably be a good dog guide. Part of Smokie's reputation came from his parents; "the apple does not fall far from the tree." I asked the trainer what specific characteristics of dog guides come from breeding.

> Well, you know, things like strong will and confidence. There are also things like lack of fear of loud noises and stuff. Of course, also intelligence. He's got the blood line. He's smart enough to learn dog guide work.

Smokie had the "right stuff" and came by it naturally. As the trainer said, "I could tell, right from the beginning, the Smokester was a natural." As a natural, the trained dog guide now needs someone to guide, someone who is "naturally" suited to the dog.

Many blind persons apply to schools for dog guides, but not all are accepted. Whether one is accepted depends in part on whether trainers think they have a good dog match for him or her, and this determination is made partly on the basis of overt physical characteristics. Does the dog work quickly? Does the dog have a strong pull? Does the blind person walk quickly? Is he or she strong enough to handle a dog with a strong pull? In short, do the dog and person possess "matching" physical features? Dog guide schools also want to know whether the blind person is what they term "active." Though all dog guides work, some are understood as requiring or wanting more work than others. Do blind person and dog guide match in this respect?

Often a school finds it difficult, and sometimes impossible, to match a particular dog with a blind person. This was the case with Smokie, as we have seen. It typically takes four to six months to train a dog, but Smokie had been at the school for about a year—not because he was a "slow learner," but because the school could not find a match for him. Smokie is extremely quick and strong, and the school had not found an applicant to match his speed and strength. According to one of the trainers, Smokie was becoming "depressed." When the trainer went to the kennel to begin training his string of dogs, Smokie was always first in line at the kennel door, ready to go. But after ten or eleven months, his enthusiasm dwindled. "It's too long to be kennelled," the trainer said. "We were going to disqualify him 'cause he was in the kennel too long. We were going to find him a good home." It was at that time that I applied to the school. The trainer told me, "I got really excited when I saw your application. On paper, a great match." The match was based on overt characteristics; my walking pace was quick enough, I was strong enough to handle Smokie, and I was also very active. As the trainer told me later, "You were Smokie's last chance."

But more than overt characteristics were involved in making this great match. Personality is also introduced into the matching process and it is not couched in the rhetoric of nature and breeding. All discussion of a dog's breed and breeding is put in terms of human descriptors—a dog is intelligent, confident, curious, and so on. When a dog is described as having a "personality," it is no wonder that we often forget that it is "just a dog."

The trainer described Smokie in this way.

He loves to work. He'll work whenever you ask him to, even at two o'clock in the morning. He'll work forever. The Smokester is the kind of dog that likes new things. He's really curious. If he doesn't work a lot, he gets bored. He really needs the work. He's confident as hell and he's got a real strong will. That's why it's good that you're an active guy.

Smokie is many things, but the trainer noted only those that characterize a dog guide. He did not mention Smokie's love of children, for example. Because of Smokie's speed I wear out about three pairs of running shoes a year, and one day I was purchasing new ones. The clerk brought me a pair of shoes, which I put on and began to lace up. Just then, I heard licking, followed by the laughter of a child. In order to lace up the shoes, I had let go of Smokie's leash, which he took as an occasion to lick the child sitting on the chair next to me. I laughed and asked him to lie down. He did, but on his way down he gave the clerk kneeling in front of my chair a quick lick.

The trainer continued his description of Smokie.

He's the kind of guy, you know, he just doesn't need much praise. But you should still praise him. You also gotta stay on top of him all the time. He's strong-willed, you know. He thinks he knows the best way of doing things. You gotta show him who's boss, or else he won't respect you.

In this description of Smokie's personality, the trainer implicitly characterized Smokie's reputation. It was no accident that Smokie and I were matched with each other. Our respective personalities were a cogent feature in making this match, arguably the most salient feature of all. After all, Smokie and I did not match in terms of species or breed, let alone blood line. Given roughly matching levels of activity and physical fitness, "personality" is the criterion trainers consider when matching dog guides with blind people.

The school I attended had its own way of describing a dog's personality, which it shared with some but not all other schools. My school invoked the polarity of "hard dogs" and "soft dogs." All dogs were interpreted as belonging to or tending toward one of these two categories. Smokie, for example, was a hard dog. Again, Smokie's trainer:

> You have to remember that Smokie is a hard dog. He's not going to freak out when you correct him. He won't get depressed for an hour after a correction. Soft dogs will. Soft dogs will, you know, mope after you correct them. Some of them, you can't even correct. They won't respond. Just a nice quiet "no" and that's enough. But Smokie is hard. Nothing bothers him. In fact, when he makes a mistake, you really have to correct him hard. You need a strong leash correction and a real hard "No!". Right after the correction, he's fine. No moping, nothing. You have to let him know with your voice, real strong voice, real loud. You have to let him know when he has made a mistake. If you don't, you know, he'll think he can just get away with it.

Smokie's reputation as a "hard dog" goes along with his identity as strong-willed and confident. If I didn't take charge, Smokie would. The trainer continued:

Smokie won't wait around for you to make a decision. You know, soft dogs, they'll just stand there forever until you tell them what to do. When you get off a bus or a subway the soft dog will just stand there till you say left or right. Not Smokie. If you wait too long, he'll decide for you. You have to be decisive. Smokie has got a real strong personality.

From the trainer's point of view, Smokie's strong personality demanded that he be matched with an even stronger one. A person with an equally strong personality would not suffice; it had to be stronger. This belief signifies how the dog as nature is present even in discussions of "personality." The trainer never forgets that Smokie is "just a dog"; as nature, Smokie must be dominated and controlled. If not, Smokie will do what he thinks best, and that may include something other than guide work. Left to decide for himself what is best, he may simply follow his natural inclinations, behaving like a dog rather than a dog guide. Thus nature is reworked by trainers into personality; it is the human conception of, and connection to, nature that allows them to make sense of dogs.

As a hard dog, Smokie is inclined to obey a strong master. His first and strongest master is nature. Any other master will have to be deserving and earn Smokie's obedience and respect by demonstrating its dominance over the mastery of nature. In contrast, the "soft dog" is more willing to accept a master other than nature. If the human master is "too strong," however, the "soft" dog returns to the comfort of nature. Either way, soft or hard, the dog returns to *its self* if the human is too hard or too soft. Expressed in human terms, a dog's personality is always a human interpretation that tacitly invokes the dog as nature and the human as existing in relation to nature. This is why all depictions of a dog, from its breeding to its personality, are dialectically tied to nature.

Trainers always treat personality, however, as a concretely knowable feature of the dog, and as the most relevant characteristic for matching dog guide with blind person. The application for dog guide school testifies to this. Dog guide schools are, of course, concerned that applicants possess the basic qualifications—"proof" of blindness (a report from an ophthalmologist), an appropriate level of physical fitness (a medical report from a physician), and an appropriate level of mobility (a report from a certified orientation and mobility instructor). But these reports on their own do not qualify an applicant to enter a training program. What tips the balance is personality. Every dog guide school orients part of its application to evaluating the personality of the applicant. Some schools interview the applicant, and all schools ask the applicant to provide personal references. Schools use these interviews and references to determine both whether the applicant's personality is generally suited to using a dog guide and whether there is an appropriate dog match available![11]

This person-dog team represents the "teaming" of nature and human through the interpretive device of personality. The realm of dog guide work presupposes the possibility of such teaming and its practices and procedures are oriented to finding the "right" individuals to form this team. The imagined relation between nature and humanity presupposed by dog guide work is expressed in this idea of the "team." Although a species, whether dog or human, is not assumed to possess a particular personality, individual representatives of the species are. As species, dogs and people are understood as co-habiting, but they only co-exist as a *team* through the invocation of personality.[12] This conception of the tie between nature and humanity is not restricted to dog guide trainers. It is an imagined relation ubiquitous in our society, and it is expressed in what I have been calling "reputation."

CONFIDENCE AND TRUST

Dog guides are reputed to possess personalities conducive to a special kind of cooperative connection between nature and humanity, and many of the comments Smokie and I hear express this idea of reputation. We often have to make quick and tricky maneuvers, especially in busy downtown areas. On one such occasion, Smokie had to work especially hard to get us to the curb at a street crossing. As we waited for the traffic light, a man said, "Well, that's really amazing. You've got quite a dog there. I can't even get my dog to heel properly."

On another occasion, Smokie and I made our way into a café, where I asked Smokie to find us a table. The café was crowded and it was made up of two levels separated by six stairs. The finesse with which Smokie found the table impressed even me. I ordered a coffee and asked the waiter if he could bring Smokie some water, which he did. A few minutes later, I heard a woman saying, "Excuse me." Because the café was crowded and I could hear many voices, I was not sure if she was talking to me. She said again, "Excuse me, is that a Black Lab?" Restraining a laugh, I told her it was, and when she asked me his name I told her this too. She told me that she had a Black

Lab, also a male, and we agreed that Black Labs are great dogs. She said she would like to pat Smokie but knew he was a working dog and that she should not do so. "It's tempting, but I know I'm not supposed to touch him." She knew the "rules," she said. I knew she was not trying to instruct me as to the "rules"; I was the one with the dog guide, after all, and she must have assumed that I knew them. She was trying to tell me that she knew something about dog guides. She continued:

> I know they have to have confidence to be trained like that. I saw you come in and it was amazing how he took you through this crowded place. He wasn't at all distracted by the crowd. He even stopped at the stairs. Then he found this table for you. You know, there's only two empty tables in this place. He's just very confident. Mine isn't. My dog would freak in a place this crowded. He's smart and everything but he's a little shy. He could never be a seeing-eye dog.

After saying that Smokie was a gorgeous dog and apologizing for the interruption, the woman excused herself and disappeared into the midst of the café.

Both of these people understood that more than training is required for dog guide work. The man's remark that he couldn't even make his dog heel properly spoke to his knowledge that all dogs do not respond equally to training. The woman's shy Black Lab, smart as he was, lacked the confidence for guide work; she understood that breed and intelligence alone do not make a good dog guide. The reputation of a "dog guide," then, relies heavily on the notion of personality, in the view not only of trainers but also of laypersons. This is not surprising, since the notion of personality in our culture is often connected to the idea of work. We often attribute personality types to particular professions and certain kinds of work. "Aptitude testing," for example, is based in part on the connection between personality and work. Humans extend this connection to non-humans, first by conceiving the dog guide as working, and second by attributing a personality type to dogs who do this work.

This connection demonstrates the human interest in the individuation of nature. Without such individuation, the possibility of dog guides would not exist. My life with Smokie cannot be captured solely within the heuristic dichotomy of human/non-human animal. In order for Smokie to guide me, I must trust him. I must trust his species as a species with the potential to guide and I must trust his breed as a breed possessing the same potential. Ultimately, however, my trust is in Smokie himself, an individual dog with a particular personality. It is this conceptual framework that provides for the possibility of trust.

The same framework also provides for the possibility of cruelty to animals. Wolfe (1993, 87), for example, argues,

> If humans use their imaginative powers to create monuments of lasting meaning out of the raw materials given to them by nature, there will often be a conflict between living by the principle of doing no harm to animals and the principle of living an imaginative and richly meaningful life. The capacity to create meaning does not come without unfairness. Because making something a symbol involves objectifying it, treating it as something other than it is, interpretation is never innocent; some will be

treated instrumentally so that others will live in a richer
and more imaginative world. Animal rights theorists are
thus correct to detect certain patterns of cruelty in the
way we use other species to make our own lives more
rich with meaning.

Trust and cruelty spring from the same source—the ob-
jectification of nature and the instrumental treatment of
its individual members.

When Smokie is guiding me, I trust his judgment, his
decisions, and his abilities. I also trust his loyalty to me. I
am trusting my interpretation of Smokie as a "working"
animal, as an animal with a job to do. Unlike most human workers, Smokie is always loyal to his work, will work
for free, will work to please me, will work because he is
bonded to me. I interpret it as "natural" to Smokie to do
these things. He gives me a richer and more imaginative
world. Whether this is actually Smokie's intention or not,
I treat it as decisive on his part. This interpretation, trusting as it is, permits me to use Smokie to enrich my own
life. Very often as I work him, I feel the presence of cruelty when Smokie breathes car exhaust fumes, burns his
feet on salted winter streets, and breathes smoke and
other fumes while we sit in bars and cafés. Very often I
think how "unnatural" this must be to Smokie.

THE EYES OF THE BOND

The idea of trust raises one final aspect of a dog guide's
identity, namely the dog's reputed ability to "bond" with
a human. The idea of bonding is grounded in the social
conception of the dog's reputation for loyalty, especially
loyalty to one "master." It is often held that a dog may

enjoy and obey several people, an entire family for example, but that the bond of loyalty is with one person only. All dogs are reputed to have this bonding capacity, dog guides especially so.

By way of illustration, I recently purchased a television (the reaction evoked by a blind person buying a television was humorous and interesting in its own right). At one point the salesperson asked me if he could pat Smokie. I explained that Smokie was in his harness, and therefore working, and that it was not a good idea for others to touch him. The salesperson apologized profusely and said,

> Dogs are great. They are so loyal. They're better than people. Even your closest friend isn't as loyal. You can always count on the dog but not always on a friend. No matter what, they're loyal. And, I bet ya that your dog is even more loyal than other dogs. They're the best friends to have.

Even though loyalty is an exclusively human concept, dogs are reputed to be more loyal even than people— the inventors of the concept. The same is true for friendship. A dog's friendship is firm and solid; you can count on it, no matter what. Loyalty must be understood within the human/nature distinction. The view that dogs are more loyal to humans than humans are to one another brings to mind the idea of the servant. People are not intrinsically viewed as servants; this is why human servants are either paid or enslaved. A dog's loyalty, however, is grounded in an understanding of nature as servant. Nature is there to serve humanity, and dogs, as nature, may be understood instrumentally as servants, and furthermore as "naturally loyal" servants. Such a conception can lead to either good stewardship or cruelty.

The dog guide harness signifies an even greater degree of loyalty and friendship. The harness suggests a "very special" bond between dog and blind person. As we were leaving the appliance shop, the salesperson said, "Boy, you can tell, you two have a very special bond." Presumably this interpretation of the "special" bond between us was part of the salesperson's interpretive scheme before he encountered Smokie and me. It was a pre-existing sense-making device. See a dog guide and blind person, see a special bond.

A friend of mine had a similar experience. She was standing on a subway platform with her dog guide, Ultra, sitting by her side. A stranger approached her and said it was clear that there was a very special bond between the two of them. My friend was not sure what would elicit such a remark, since Ultra was simply sitting beside her. Clearly, the stranger was looking at my friend and Ultra through the eyes of the "bond" they were presumed to share. The dog guide is reputed to be bonded to a blind person, and no matter what the woman on the platform saw, she would have seen this presumed bond. Those of us who use dog guides share this understanding of the bond with our dogs as an ultimate form of closeness. Chevigny (1946, 210) expresses the matter this way:

> For they have an apt phrase at Seeing Eye: the dog doesn't belong to you, you belong to the dog. The month you spend training there is none too long a period for, to be successful with your dog, before you leave the place you must have won his affection and co-operation in a way that has never before been done with a dog on earth.

The relationship between man and dog is as old as written history, but it remained for Seeing Eye to bring it to its ultimate closeness.

Thus the bond binds not only dog and person, it also binds the species, breed, training, and personality necessary for success into the "team."

The idea of the bond is an essential feature of dog guide training as well. In fact, the presupposed ability of dogs to bond to people and vice versa is one reason why dogs are used for guiding. Dog guide trainers also work with the assumption that a dog guide will only work well with a blind person if the two are bonded.

I spent the first two days at the dog guide school without a dog. I did not even meet Smokie in these first days. The trainers had two reasons for this. For one thing, we students needed to learn about dogs and dog guides. We needed to learn how to use the harness and what to expect when the harness was on the dog; the trainers stood in for the dogs in these exercises. These two days also gave the trainers the opportunity to evaluate the appropriateness of the matches they had made on paper. On the third morning the trainers met with us and announced:

After this meeting, you'll all go back to your rooms. At ten o'clock we'll bring you your dogs. So wait in your rooms and your dogs will be there at ten. From then till lunchtime we want you to be in your rooms with your dogs. At twelve o'clock, harness them up and come downstairs for lunch. You need to spend these two hours bonding with them. This is very important. Remember, your dogs have gone through a lot. At first, they were bonded to their mother and litter mates and then we took them away. We took them to a foster family for about a year. Of course, they bonded to the family. Then we brought them back to the kennel for training. They were here from anywhere from six months to a year. During that time, they bonded to us trainers. Now they have to bond to you. They bonded three times and now they have to bond again. It's hard on them. They had to break at least three bonds. So, remember, it's really important to bond. If your dog is going to work for you, you're going to have to bond. It can be the best-trained dog in the world but without a bond, forget it. Also, your dogs want to work, they love it. They want to bond with you. So get to know them in your rooms for a couple of hours. Play with them. Okay, that's it. You can go to your rooms now and you'll get your dog in a couple of minutes. See you in the lunch room at twelve.

This was, without a doubt, the most exciting yet apprehensive moment I experienced at the school. I was flooded with nervousness and eager anticipation at the prospect of finally meeting such a highly admired animal. The apprehension I felt centered on the idea of the dog's reputation.[13] I was about to receive a fully trained dog guide. My dog would know exactly what to do, but I would not. Other than following a trainer around with a harness, I did not know how to work a dog guide, and I was about to apprentice with a master. The feeling I had was enormously ominous. I was about to meet not "just a dog," but a dog who loved to work, who wanted to work, and who wanted to bond with me. I was in awe. How would I treat such a dog? What would I do when I met him? Would I embarrass myself? Did I have what it takes to work with this dog? These questions and many more raced through my mind as I made my way to my room to await the arrival of my dog.

I was sitting on my bed when the trainer arrived at the door with my dog. He knocked and, without entering, said "I have your dog. His name is Smokie and I'm opening your door and letting him in now." The door opened and in ran Smokie. The whole room was filled with energy and excitement. Smokie jumped on me, and for all my excitement I remembered something the trainer had told us. "Don't let your dog up on your bed or any other furniture. If you do that, he'll think he can go on furniture anywhere." As I was sitting on the bed when Smokie jumped on me, I immediately said "Off." That was the first word I spoke to the master. Smokie's momentum carried him from me onto the bed, across it, and off the other side. The trainer said "Good," and left Smokie and me in our room. At the time, I was convinced that it was my command "off," and not Smokie's momentum, that carried him off the bed. I learned then how suggestively strong a reputation can be.

In sum, the ideas of species, breed, training, personality, and bond make up the reputation of the dog guide. All of these elements are the result of human interpretations of nature. We conceive of ourselves as both apart from and a part of nature, and our relationship with nature runs the interpretive gamut from dominance over it to dependence on it to harmonious living in it. One thing is certain; all conceptions of nature are decisively human. The dog guide team represents one such decisive relation to nature.

CHAPTER SIX

Feel Free to Ask

"Do you know where you are?"
—WOMAN ON A SUBWAY CAR

S O FAR I HAVE tried to depict the elements which, in combination, produce a dog guide's identity. This is not merely a heuristic enterprise. Both identity and reputation play themselves out in everyday life. They are formed and re-formed through social interaction. Let us now take a closer look at identity and reputation "at work."

People ask me many questions about Smokie and our life and work together. As might be expected, some are intelligent questions that spring from genuine curiosity, while others seem to come from an exaggerated sense of Smokie's reputation. "How long did it take to train him?" and "How long did it take you to learn to work with him?" are genuinely curious questions and presuppose that to become a guide, a dog must be trained in a different way and for a longer time than a dog in typical obedience training is. They also presuppose that the blind person must be trained to work with the dog, but otherwise they do not "answer themselves" by an exaggerated sense of reputation.

Other types of questions, while also genuine and possibly even curious, carry with them an exaggerated sense of Smokie's reputation. These questions and comments usually come in the form of compliments. I was working Smokie on a busy downtown street one day when I felt, through his harness, his head move quickly down. He raised it almost immediately and picked up his pace a little. I knew that he had either bent to sniff something or had succumbed to the temptation of checking out a discarded piece of food. I was about to praise him for realizing that he had made a mistake when I heard someone say, "Look at that, the dog's making sure that the guy doesn't walk in anything dangerous." Smokie had done no such thing. But to that person, a dog in harness is always responsible and forever vigilant.

Smokie's reputation is reflected in other ways. I am constantly asked questions about his ability to tell whether a traffic light is in our favor. Many people assume he can do so, but they want to know how. Sometimes I tell them the truth and say that Smokie cannot tell whether the light is in our favor. I make that judgment, and when I judge that the traffic light is in our favor I give Smokie the command "forward." Smokie then decides whether it is safe for us to cross the street or not. He will obey me, but only if it is safe.

Then there are other times—times when I am in a particularly good mood or when the question is asked in a overly serious way or when I am interested in just how far people are willing to stretch Smokie's reputation—when I answer differently. Smokie and I had been walking for approximately thirty minutes on our way to the university. We stopped at a curb and were waiting for the light to change. It was very busy and there was a lot of traffic, so it was easy for me to tell when the light changed. As we waited, a man who was also waiting said that he had been following us for many blocks and was amazed by how quickly we walked and how gracefully—that was his word—Smokie took me around obstacles and pedestrians. But what most amazed him was that Smokie knew when the traffic light was in our favor. "I just can't get over how your dog knows when the light is green," he said.

I should note that Smokie responds to both verbal commands and hand signals. I told the man that I was equally amazed by Smokie's ability but that I did not know how he did it either. When the traffic flow told me that the light had changed, I gave Smokie a quick and unobtrusive hand signal indicating forward. Smokie stepped off the curb. I turned back to the man and said "See, there he goes. I don't know how he does it." As Smokie and I proceeded quickly across the street, I heard the man behind me say, "That's amazing!"

On another occasion, Smokie and I were proceeding down the street toward a particular address. Because I teach courses in that building, we go there several times a week, and Smokie knows where the door is. Whenever we pass any familiar place, Smokie will hesitate in order to let me know that we are there and to ask whether or not that is where I want to go. If I do not respond, he continues down the street. A simple "good" from me and Smokie turns to the door.

As we approached the place, I heard a male voice behind me repeatedly calling "Sir." Finally I asked Smokie to stay and turned to ask the man whether he was speaking to me. By this time, the man was by my side. He said that he was impressed by how Smokie guided me, by how he "took me around." He said it looked as if Smokie knew exactly where he was going. "It must make you feel great knowing that all you have to do is tell your dog where you wanna go and he'll take you right there." He then asked me where I was going.

I told him I was trying to find the address 151 on that street. He said that it was just up the street a little. I told him that Smokie had no difficulty in finding even-numbered addresses but that he was not quite as adept at finding addresses with odd numbers. The man asked me if I would like him to help. I suggested that he could follow behind us and let me know whether or not Smokie turned into the door marked 151; he agreed. I then said "Forward Smokie. Find 1-5-1." Of course, when we reached the correct address, the familiar building, Smokie hesitated. I whispered "good" and he turned toward the door. After asking Smokie to "stay," I turned to the man and asked "Is this it? Did he get it right?" "I can't believe it!" the man replied. "He did it! You know, that's amazing!" I suggested that maybe Smokie was getting better at recognizing odd numbers. After thanking the man for his help, Smokie and I entered the building.

In instances such as these, the reputation of the dog guide takes on an almost supernatural quality. Some people will attribute almost any ability, animal or human, to the dog guide. More often than one would guess, Smokie's reputation allows him to be seen as almost completely removed from animal nature and endowed with human reason and motivation. This transformation takes place in the minds of those who have an exalted conception of Smokie's reputation as a dog guide. What is interesting is that people are "amazed" by their own creative projections. Some people are "mystified" by the abilities of dog guides, abilities that exist only through their own creations. As Marx might say, we create and are then mystified by our creations.

THE IDENTITY AND REPUTATION OF THE TEAM

So far, I have been speaking about the reputation of the dog guide as if it is attributed almost exclusively to the dog. This is only partly true, of course. The reputation of the dog guide is fashioned in combination with conceptions of blindness. Although I have implied such a connection, I have not interrogated it directly. Let me now do so.

As in the case of the dog guide, some people have an exaggerated view of the abilities of blind persons. It is commonly believed that we have better hearing than sighted persons, that we possess a "sixth sense," that we have "insights" that no sighted person could have, that we are unemployable and live in poverty, that we need help, and, of course, that we are all musically inclined. These things are undoubtedly true of some blind persons but also of some persons who see. Whatever the actual case, our society does form collective representations of blindness and uses them as a way to "see" blind persons and as a way to make sense of their appearance in society. The reputation of a dog guide is informed by these collective representations of blindness, for without a blind person there is no dog guide. Conceptions of the dog and blind person are used, often tacitly, to construct the identity and reputation of the "dog guide team."

The reputation of the dog guide alone tends to be positive to an exaggerated degree. But any flaw or failing perceived in the dog guide's ability is typically blamed not on the dog but on its blind partner. I recently had my hair cut in a salon I have patronized for almost two years. I know all of the stylists and all of them know me and Smokie. They all like and admire Smokie and are always glad to see him. On this occasion, one of the stylists told me of a woman who had been there earlier in the week with her dog guide. She said that the dog "wasn't like Smokie at all."

> This blind woman bumped into everything. The dog couldn't even find her the chair. And then it wouldn't just lie down quietly like Smokie does. After, if you can believe it, she asked if one of us could take her out to the streetcar stop. The dog couldn't even do that. I don't think she knows what to do with that dog. She doesn't seem to know how to use it. She's sure not like you and Smokie.

This dog guide team was not living up to its reputation. The employees of this salon, it is true, have based their view of dog guides in part on their experience with Smokie, who is in every way a superior dog guide. Nonetheless, the woman and her dog were not doing what dog guide teams are reputed to be able to do.

The stylist blamed this on the incompetence of the blind woman. Her standard in this judgment was the reputation she attributes to dog guide teams in general and to Smokie and me in particular. No fault, however, was attributed to the dog. The blind woman was solely responsible for any incompetence.

> You know, it can't be the dog's fault. I mean, it's just a dog. It's trained to do what it's supposed to do but then

it's up to the person to get it to do that. She never does anything when it makes a mistake. You know, she bumps into a chair but then doesn't say anything to the dog. How's the dog supposed to know? I suppose, sometimes, some dogs just aren't cut out for that kind of work. But this is ridiculous. I mean it's trained. Why have a dog like that if someone has to take you everywhere?

The stylist did raise the possibility that this particular dog might not be suited to guide work, but then quickly dismissed this possibility. After all, the dog was "trained," and if the dog was not suited to guiding, this surely would have been discovered during the training process. The fault, then, must lie with the blind person and how she handles her dog. In this case, the dog's reputation was tarnished by the blind person. The dog guide was doing its part, but the blind person was not.

Note that the stylist said nothing about the woman's training. Like her dog, the woman was also trained but the stylist ignored this, making an implicit distinction between animal and human training.[1] The stylist assumed that the dog would robotically do what it was trained to do unless the woman failed to reinforce the training, in which case it would forget. The woman had also been trained, but she, being human, was not expected to act like a robot. The stylist assumed that the woman ignored what she was trained to do. As nature, dogs have no choice but to do what they are trained to do, whereas people can choose to follow or ignore their training.

The "burden of proof" here is on blindness, not on the dog. There are times when this burden is expressed more subtly, as when the collective representation of "help" is at work. If you are blind, you must need help. There are certainly times when Smokie and I need help and when this is clear to sighted observers—for example, at intersections where the vehicular traffic is minimal. Light traffic flow makes it difficult to determine whether or not the traffic light is in our favor, and on these occasions people do ask if I need help, or they simply say "You can go." There are times when Smokie and I are looking for a particular place, say a bar. If we haven't been there before, we may experience some difficulty in finding it. Sometimes this is obvious to people, and they may ask if we need help. Of course, help is offered not only to blind persons. Anyone who appears to be lost or in trouble may be asked if they need help. But there are times when blind persons are offered help, or even given unsolicited help, when it is far from clear that they need it. Smokie and I were making our way out of a subway station and heading toward a familiar exit. Without warning, someone grabbed my arm and said, "It's this way." I shook free and said "No it isn't," and Smokie and I proceeded on our way. What the person "saw" when she saw Smokie and me was blindness and, consequently, the need for help. This incident illustrates the power of societal conceptions of blindness.

I am sometimes asked, "Do you know where you are?" or "Do you know where you're going?"—both derivatives of "Do you need help?" Our social identity is formed, in part, through the collective assumption that blind persons need help, and our appearance in the world marks an occasion to re-identify Smokie and me in this way. Once we were on our way home on a familiar subway line, one on which we both knew all the stops. Someone sat down next to us and after a few seconds asked, "Do you know where you are?" This was the first time I had ever been asked such a question, and it took me by surprise. I was sitting on the subway, Smokie was lying beside me, and we had three stops to go. What is more, the names of the stops are announced over the subway's public address system. I could not imagine what it was that Smokie and I were doing to have caused this person to wonder whether we knew where we were—unless, of course, it was the simple fact of my blindness. "See blindness; see the need for help." I decided to find out how far this person would go in her assumptions about blindness. "Where?" I asked. The person surprised me again as she proceeded to tell me which subway line we were on, the direction in which the train was going, and the name of the next stop. The woman seriously assumed that I did not know where I was. What she thought Smokie and I were doing on that subway was something I did not want to address.

Partly to enjoy the humor of this situation and partly to show the woman the folly of her concern, I asked, "What city?" After a few seconds of silence, she began to laugh. She then apologized, explaining that she had seen the dog and, in her words, "I just automatically thought you needed help. I didn't even think." She apologized again when Smokie stood, without any command from me, as the subway approached our stop. As the train stopped, she said, "I think your dog is smarter than me." By exaggerating the conception of "help" that blind persons are assumed to need, I allowed the woman to turn her gaze away from me and focus it on herself. With her quip that Smokie was smarter than she was, she let me know that she had examined her presupposition and found it wanting.

On another occasion Smokie and I were proceeding down a street on our way to meet someone at a café, when I heard a voice behind me ask "Do you know where you're going?" Not thinking the question was directed at us, Smokie and I continued our quick pace. The question came again. I asked Smokie to stay, turned, and asked, "Are you speaking to me?" The voice said, "Yeah, do you know where you're going?" I asked the person whether we looked like we did not. He responded, "Not really," and disappeared. At that point, Smokie shook himself out as dogs do, and I followed suit, shaking my head in dismay. We then proceeded to our appointment.

When I reflected on these encounters, I had to wonder: Of whom would one ask such questions? On one level, the answer was simple: We ask these questions of those who appear to be lost or in need of help. "Needing help" is a notion manifested through interaction. In an ethnomethodological sense (Garfinkel 1967), "needing help" is interactionally achieved; it is achieved reflexively through interpretation. Someone may orient an interaction to "look like" help is needed, and someone else may correspondingly interpret it as such. Together they interactionally achieve "needing help."[2]

When Smokie and I were asked these questions, we were not orienting our interaction to express the need for help, but we were nonetheless interpreted that way. We, or more correctly I, must have been interpreted as the "type" who needed help. When someone is interpreted in this way, it is interactionally reasonable to offer help. Strangers, tourists, children, and elderly people are often understood as needing help. Blind persons are often interpreted as fitting this interpretive schema, regardless of whether we actively express this need. It is very unlikely that someone who appears able to see, someone walking confidently down a city sidewalk, has ever been asked if they knew where they were.

The dog guide team signifies that the human member of that team is blind. Despite the presence of this "team," however, interaction is often informed by collective representations of blindness alone. The team may be viewed from the standpoint of the "teaming" of competence and incompetence. Simply put, the dog can "get around" on its own; the blind person cannot, or there would be no need for a dog guide. The presence of a dog guide always represents the incompetence of a blind person in relation to mobility, though this "incompetence" is often couched in the more positive political language of "disability" or "challenge." But even this "politically correct" language implies incompetence and the need for help. The dog is always interpreted as the competent member, as the one with the "good reputation." The blind person is always interpreted as incompetent, as the one with the "stigma" (Goffman, 1963a).

That the blind person needs help is one collective representation of blindness, but there are others, such as "all blind persons live in poverty." After a busy morning, Smokie and I needed a break and I decided to stop for coffee. We were in an area of the city with which we had only a passing familiarity, but friends had told me of an interesting café there, and I knew I could get close to it. My plan was to get as near the café as we could and then to ask someone for directions. After a few minutes of walking, I asked Smokie to stay and we stopped. I asked a passerby if he could tell me where the Free Times café was, and he said it was just two doors down. I thanked

him and was about to give Smokie the command "forward," when the helpful passerby asked if I intended to
have lunch there. I told him I just wanted coffee. He said,
"Well, even coffee's expensive in there," and told me of
a doughnut shop around the corner where I could get a
cheap coffee. Before I could respond, he disappeared.
Smokie and I proceeded into Free Times, where he had
free water and I had expensive coffee.

Later that same week, Smokie and I were standing on
a street waiting for a friend. We were outside a shop just
to the right of the door, I standing and Smokie sitting on
my left side. As we waited, a man took my right hand,
saying "There you go," and walked away. He had placed
a one-dollar coin in my hand. Later, I tried to give the
coin to a "street person" whom I overheard asking for
spare change. At first he refused, saying that I probably
needed it more than he did. After assuring him that I did
not need the coin, he finally accepted it.

To see a blind person as unable to afford coffee at an
up-scale café is one societal expression of the view of
blind persons as "poor." So too is seeing a blind person
standing on the street as a beggar. The conception of
blindness in terms of poverty is connected to the interpretation that blind persons require help. What blind
persons need help with are the *conditions of life* that blindness generates, and poverty is typically understood as
one such condition. This view of blindness recommends
cheaper cafés and bestows dollar coins.

As Smokie and I left the Free Times café that day, I was
feeling a little "down," wondering if blindness would
ever be seen in a more positive light by my society. I felt
like I was fighting an uphill battle, and it was becoming
quite tiresome. I was not in the best of moods, but I had

one more stop to make before heading home. I needed to purchase three copies of a book.

Smokie and I made our way to the bookstore, entered, and proceeded up the escalator to the second floor. I asked Smokie to find the counter, and when we arrived at it I asked him to lie down. He did and I waited at the counter, which was chest high, for service. In a few moments, a clerk asked if he could help me. I told him the title of the book I was looking for. He said that it was downstairs in the Literary Criticism section. I thanked him and asked Smokie to stand. I grasped the handle and said, "Forward Smoke. Find the escalator." Upon noticing Smokie, the clerk said, "Hey, you've got a dog." I asked Smokie to stay, turned to the clerk, and said, "I know." The clerk laughed and said, "I guess you do." He offered to come downstairs and find the book for me. I told him that this was not necessary, but he insisted, so I said, "Great."

Smokie and I arrived at the escalator before the clerk did and he followed us downstairs. I then asked Smokie to stay and told the clerk that if he led the way Smokie would follow. "He will?" asked the clerk. I asked Smokie to follow the man, and we did. A few seconds later, Smokie stopped. I put my foot out and felt a stair. I said, "Good boy, forward," and we went down the three stairs.

Turning back to us, the clerk said, "Jeez, where'd you go?" I told him that Smokie had stopped for the stairs. "Right," he said, "I forgot to tell ya." "That's okay," I replied, "that's what I've got him for." "He's smart," said the clerk, and I agreed. The clerk gave a short laugh and so did I. He said, "I guess I didn't have to tell you where the stairs were," and we laughed harder. Still laughing, the clerk said I could wait where I was and he would get the book. I waited, wondering why this situation seemed so amusing. In a few seconds the clerk was back with the book. "Found it. I guess I'm pretty smart too." Our laughter became uncontrollable giggling. Through the giggling, I told him that I had forgotten but that I needed two more copies. The clerk said, "If he's so smart, let him find you the books." Almost in hysterics, he added, "You know, you can read one book more than once, you don't need three." "Really?" I replied. "You'd think someone would have told me that before."

In a few moments the clerk handed me three copies of the book. Through his laughter, he asked, "Does he read these books for you too?" "Only the ones with pictures," I said. Still laughing, I thanked him for his help. He asked if I needed help finding the cashier. I told him that I could manage and, still laughing, we said our goodbyes. I paid for the books and Smokie and I left the store.

The irony of a blind person not only being in a book store but buying books struck us both as funny. As much as Smokie "sees for me," books are outside of his "realm of vision." This may have been the source of the humor that the clerk and I used as a response to the irony of my buying books. Whatever its source, I no longer felt down, and the uphill battle I had been waging was over for the moment.

THE REFLEXIVITY OF IDENTITY AND REPUTATION

The reputation of the dog guide and stereotypes of blindness—conceptions we hold whether we have had direct experience with them or not—work together to form our impressions of the dog guide team. We carry these impressions with us and they inform both our literal perception of such a team and what we make of that perception. Reputation and stereotype precede direct experience; they allow us to recognize and make sense of experience. At the same time, experience reflexively influences and enhances reputation and stereotype.

The work of Mannheim helps in understanding this reflexive interpretive process.

> The degree of objectification possible is dependent upon the particular meta-logical and primitive "given" we wish to pick out from the "flow of experience" for the purpose of objectification. Every meaning refers to something—and the further this something is from being completely objectifiable, the more intimately it is bound up with the stream of experience from which it is raised to the object-status, the more subjective, also, will be the corresponding meanings. Meanings always clearly show a greater or lesser degree of objectivity in that they are more or less intimately bound up with the "flow of experience," and it is always possible to ascertain this degree of objectivity by inspecting them. (Mannheim, 1953, 57)

When the "flow of experience" includes the experience of a dog guide team, meaning is given to it by an interpretive "meta-logic" and a presupposed "given." The viewer brings with him or her the implicit interpretive schema of the dog guide team. The actual experience is "seen" through this meta-logic and preconceived schema and is thus objectified, or picked out from the flow of subjective experience and transformed into the perceived "object" of the dog guide team.

While this perception is objective in the narrow sense that the eyes distinguish a person holding a harness that is attached to a dog, the meaning of what is seen remains embedded in the viewer's preconceived notions, in the subjective "stream of experience" with which it is inevitably bound up. The dog guide team "stands out" in this stream since it is not an everyday sight in the experience of most people; it is "radically" noticeable in the way that a celebrity is. Smokie's presence forces all eyes on us.

Following Mannheim, Garfinkel conceives of this interpretive process as a method that we tacitly employ in seeing and achieving a sensible, objective world. This "documentary method of interpretation" consists of

> treating an actual appearance as "the document of," as "pointing to," as "standing on behalf of" a presupposed underlying pattern. Not only is the underlying pattern derived from its individual documentary evidence, but the individual documentary evidence, in their turn, are interpreted on the basis of "what is known" about the underlying pattern. Each is used to elaborate the other. (Garfinkel, 1967, 78)

What people know about dog guides and how they experience them derives from this meta-logical "underlying pattern" of preconceptions. The actual experience of a dog guide team "points to" this underlying pattern, which enables a sensible and recognizable object to emerge. The underlying pattern of the dog guide is what I have been calling its "reputation" and, as we have seen, this reputation often says more about the human observer than it does about the dog guide. The idea of reputation is part of the gestalt of meaning and the web of interpretation that mark and define the "flow of experience" that Smokie and I have in public.

The preconceptions that people bring to their observations of dog guides and the behavior they witness in an actual dog guide elaborate one another, but one does not necessarily transform the other. The man who believed that Smokie could read street numbers was prepared to believe this fiction because of his exalted conception of the dog guide's reputed abilities and intelligence. It is true that I encouraged him in this belief, but he failed to get the joke, so firm were his preconceptions of the dog guide. The man who believed Smokie could gauge the changing of a traffic light was similarly influenced by his own preconceptions. It is true that dog guides are intelligent and talented, and have been trained to do things that merely "natural" dogs cannot, and both of these observers had witnessed Smokie guiding me with grace and competence. But their exaggerated notions of the dog guide's talents allowed them to believe something that flew in the face of reason.

Simple ignorance also plays a part in people's perceptions of and behavior toward dog guides. People often whistle at Smokie or call "here boy"; sometimes they even try to pat him. I always ask or tell people not to do this, explaining that it might be distracting and potentially dangerous. People typically plead ignorance in such cases. Smokie and I were waiting at a busy intersection, both very focused and attentive, for the traffic light to turn. A woman began to pat Smokie, saying, "You're such a smart dog. You know, I really love dogs." I asked her to stop touching Smokie, as he was working, and she immediately apologized, saying, "Oh, I didn't know. I didn't know you couldn't touch seeing eye dogs." On another occasion, Smokie and I boarded a crowded street-car, and I asked Smokie to find me a seat. As he maneuvered us through the streetcar, a man began touching him and said, "Wow, you're a great dog, aren't you?" I said, "Please don't touch him, he's working." "Aren't you supposed to touch these dogs?" was his response. Neither of these people apparently counted "potential to be distracted" among the dog guide's reputed list of traits.

Distraction is not a response restricted to dog guides, of course. All sorts of things distract all sorts of people, and there are times when we are not aware that we are distracting others. Humming a tune in a library, for example, may be distracting to some, but the person humming may be unaware that she is humming. But there are other things that a reasonable person should know are distracting without having to be told—patting a working dog guide in the middle of a busy intersection, for example.

The dog guide's exaggerated reputation as "expert," however, "blinds" some people to what should be obvious. People who distract dog guides see themselves as "laypeople" in relation to the expert. They are uninformed; they don't know the "rules," and indeed sometimes they invoke a legitimate excuse for their ignorance, such as simple lack of experience with an actual dog guide team. When they are informed—for example, that one should not touch a dog guide in harness—they incorporate this new information into their conception of the dog guide; henceforth part of the dog guide's reputation in that person's "underlying pattern" is that the dog must be respected and left alone when it is working. People elaborate their preconceptions in this way by asking *any* expert about the particulars of their work.

It is the interpretive category of "reputation" that precedes Smokie and me. Reputation is a sense-making device (Garfinkel, 1967) for all members of social settings. We are all involved in a tacit process of interpretation that makes our presence and that of others in a given setting appear reasonable and sensible. As a rule, we see nothing out of the ordinary in a public place. We see people, but often do not notice them. They are "just there" in the way everyone is just there in a public place. But the story is different for Smokie and me. We are extraordinary insofar as a dog guide team is an out-of-the-ordinary experience in a public place. As a sighted friend said to me as we were walking down the street, "All eyes are on you and Smokie."

As Mannheim might say, my experience with Smokie provides an occasion for me to notice and consequently inspect the reputations and presupposed underlying patterns that precede all of us in our day-to-day lives. "Having a reputation" by itself does not teach us anything unless we notice and inspect it, but when we do, we learn something. Life with Smokie provides me with such opportunities all the time.

For the past five years, my identity has been inexorably bound to Smokie. The bond of which dog trainers and other "dog experts" speak pales in comparison to the bond that binds Smokie and me. We are alone together in our identities and this togetherness binds them into "our identity." Together and separate we are alone and alone we are one.

This may be an expression of a sentiment but it is not sentimental in the usual sense. The reputation that springs from Smokie's identity certainly has sentiment as one of its features. We often evoke smiles and even sentimental looks from others as we make our way through our world. But our identity, alone together, resists whatever preconceptions others may have of us. The influence of others is expressed in how we interact with them, but our identity is firm. It holds fast and our bond remains, through all situations, the bond of a secure identity. Smokie and I have no "identity crisis" as we move through our world.

The way we move through our world is, in fact, a defining feature of our identity. Our grace of independence, alone together, is a noticeable and even a remarkable thing to many. To us, our grace is not so much noticed as it is lived and known. Smokie and I have achieved an identity which no longer depends on being alone and is not yet a complete togetherness of man and dog. It is an "alone-together" which is always marked by my aloneness in humanity and Smokie's aloneness in nature, which come together in the bond of identity.

We represent the inseparable character of the alone-together relationship. We live between aloneness and togetherness and thus our unity represents the enigma and mystery of being different from one another and yet the same. But what is the nature of this relation between Smokie and me and between nature and society?

CHAPTER SEVEN

The Two-In-One

"What distinguishes men from animals is born
of our relationship with them."
—JOHN BERGER, *ABOUT LOOKING*

THIS WORK IS my attempt to depict my life with
Smokie, which I have characterized as a relationship based on the idea of the "alone-together."
The alone-together suggests that we possess unity with
each other as well as separateness from each other. Our
separateness, or difference from each other, originates
and is steeped in the distinction between nature and humanity. However else we are together, we are first and
foremost "man and dog." We are distinct from one another not simply on the basis that we are two different
living creatures, but on the more fundamental level that
we are two different species. Smokie is *Canis familiaris*
and I am *Homo sapiens.* He is a representative of nature, I
of humanity. This marks our fundamental difference.

Some will not be satisfied with this distinction. They
are vexed by the question of what distinguishes humanity
from nature—in our case, what distinguishes humans
from animals. This question presupposes such a distinction, but at the same time it implies a concern for

whether or not the distinction is valid or even whether it expresses an anthropocentrism. Even though these concerns are philosophic ones, a program of empirical research has been established as a way to address them.[1] Is it the ability to think that distinguishes humans from animals? The ability to use tools? The ability to speak? The ability to control and manipulate nature? These are but a few of the questions that are raised and addressed by such research. Despite their empirical nature, the posing of these questions presupposes the distinction they are seeking. Without a distinction between humans and animals, questions about its precise character could not be asked.

The postmodern privileging of perspective influences the motivation for the asking of such questions. Animals and humans alike have a perspective that defines what is real. The postmodern slant on this is that not only are all perspectives equally valid but that any notion of reality can be gleaned only from perspective. This view results in a world of multiple realities in which every reality is as real as every other reality. To privilege one reality over another, from this standpoint, is to be guilty of egocentrism, ethnocentrism, anthropocentrism; the assertion of one reality or one "truth" over another is an illusion animated by hegemonic self-interest.

Regardless of how the distinction between humans and animals is conceived, it is based upon and expresses a relation. My understanding of Smokie, for example, is based upon such a relation. There are times when I trust his judgment more than I do that of a human. When a stranger took my arm and offered to take me through a construction site, I told him, "Let him work." I was not being anthropocentric, but distinguishing between the

guiding prowess of a person and that of Smokie—if anything, one might argue that I was guilty of anthropomor-
phism, of endowing Smokie with human attributes. It was
my relation to Smokie—my trust in his loyalty and competence in guiding—that motivated my comment.

As Berger (1980, 7) says, "What distinguishes men
from animals is born of our relationship with them." My
work, both with Smokie and in the writing of this book,
presupposes this distinction and this relationship. The
analysis presented in each of the previous chapters begins with my lived experience as a blind person and with
Smokie. That I "see" a distinction between humans and
animals is grounded in this experience. The relationship
of which this is born is crystallized in my reflections upon
this experience.

LIVING WITH BLINDNESS

I drew a distinction between living *with* blindness and living *in* blindness.[2] This distinction, like the one between
humans and animals, was also born of our relationship
with it. Whether we live with or in blindness depends on
our conception of it.

The conception of blindness as an externally motivated condition which imposes negative effects upon a
person results in a life *with* it. The notion of externality is
crucial to this concept, for it sees blindness as external
to the individual, motivated by disease, accident, or genetics. This makes blindness a condition that imposes itself indiscriminately on individuals, an inadequate physiology which should *naturally* be otherwise. The ability to
see, from this perspective, depends on a naturally func-
tioning physiology. Any "act of nature," in this view, is a

natural one and thus "mindless." Nature's actions are not based on prejudice or self-interest but are random and indiscriminate. Pollution, for example, is understood as the result of human intervention that causes not only a polluted natural environment but also a polluted version of "natural equality."

This point of view treats blindness as a condition that cannot be blamed on anyone or anything but merely *happens* to people. It is like any other "natural happening" except for one thing—it is a mistake, but a natural one. Nature possesses anomalies, exceptions to the "natural rule." Disease and flawed genes are seen as an anomaly in relation to the natural order of things. Accidents too are often understood as natural occurrences. What accident, for example, wiped out the dinosaurs over 65,000,000 years ago? Was it a giant meteor shower, or was it merely an instance of the way in which evolution naturally works?

Humanity enters the realm of naturally occurring anomalies and accidents in the exclusively human act of interpretation. Human interpretation begins with judging these anomalies as either good or bad. This judgment is based on a presupposed distinction between nature and humanity. Any effect that nature might have on itself is never interpreted as bad. Unpleasant as it may look to human eyes, for example, a lion ripping out the throat of a gazelle is seen as part of the natural order of things; it is interpreted as a good thing insofar as it enables the natural food chain to sustain itself. Even the death of weak and diseased animals is interpreted as "nature's way" of insuring the species' survival. "Nature is therefore something which as it were holds to its own course, and does so in and of itself" (Gadamer 1996, 36).

In fact, the only bad thing about nature is understood as springing from human intervention. Nature, in this view, possesses an "internal perfection" which, left to its own devices, will take care of itself, even if this process is, as yet, beyond human understanding. The workings of nature can only be seen as "bad" when human beings become part of the equation.

Natural occurrences are not always seen as so benign when they happen to human beings. People see blindness as a mistake, and even though nature, being mindless, cannot be blamed the way a person's self-interest or malice can be blamed, blindness is still seen as a bad thing. Blindness is not merely the unfortunate luck of the "natural draw"; it is the misfortune of the one who draws blindness from nature's deck.

Blindness is not an instance of natural selection and survival, but the human misfortune of having made a "bad draw." A wildebeest has no chance of winning when it draws the natural card of blindness. It must sacrifice its life in order to preserve the strength of its species. A human being who draws the "blind card," on the other hand, has a chance of winning and sacrifices a life of seeing in order to preserve the strength of the human spirit. The person who draws the blind card now focuses on playing the other cards in her or his hand—the cards of hearing, of touching, and especially of the human spirit. Bad card in hand, this person goes on to strengthen the other cards by playing them effectively. Thus humans assert themselves in nature in a way that animals do not. "As human beings we are not wholly accommodated to our natural environment through the mechanisms of instinct and reaction. Precisely this is our 'nature,' that we must assert ourselves over and against nature as far as we can" (Gadamer 1996, 139).

The card-playing metaphor depicts what I mean by living *with* blindness. Blindness is reduced to a physical condition with which one must cope and to which one must adjust. The result is a person "who happens to be blind."

Living with blindness requires a separation of an individual from his body. This separation is different from Plato's body/soul distinction or Descartes's body/mind split; it is better characterized as the body/person split. This type of dichotomy, in its modern form, derives from the Enlightenment's separation of reason (the human mind's special capability) and passion, emotion, and instinct (the primitive or animal forces). The Enlightenment's privileging of reason as the distinguishing and animating feature of humankind made the body, symbol of emotion and instinct, a separate and opposing entity. Thus the Age of Reason dichotomized nature and society, and distinguished between laws of nature and laws of society. The key to unlocking both these sets of laws was, of course, human reason.

A similar dichotomy, the body/person split, is essential for a life *with* blindness, for the life of the person "who happens to be blind." Living *with* blindness means understanding blindness as a strictly physical condition of the body—a defective and inadequate physiology of the eye. "Blind eyes" do not function as they were "naturally intended" to do, and the origin of their defect is typically situated within the paradigm of "bodily cause." When this "cause" cannot be located in the body, the person is not considered "really blind," but is suffering from some sort of psychological disorder. However, even psychosomatic blindness falls within the body/person split, as it is yet another sign of the "power of mind," albeit a "mind gone bad."

The Enlightenment's distinction between nature and society supported the belief that nature could be mastered and controlled through the use of reason and its offspring, science and technology. This leads to the interpretation of reason as knowledge and subsequently power (Foucault, 1972). The evolution of human reason, and its mastery of nature, would result in ever increasing human progress, and this belief in progress is the Enlightenment's legacy to us. Living *with* blindness is rooted in just such an understanding of humanity and nature. Human blindness may be a natural happenstance, but it can be known, understood, and to some degree mastered. It can be overcome insofar as collective social life possesses the power of reason. The same understanding does not hold when blindness occurs in a wolf or a gazelle. Natural animal creatures, lacking the power of reason and the ability to create coping technologies, cannot overcome blindness. Instead, nature destroys blindness by destroying those individual creatures "who happen to be blind." The wolf will starve to death; the gazelle will be easy prey to its predators. Living with blindness can occur *only* in human society.

Living with and overcoming blindness is manifest in a variety of ways in our society. There are optical technologies that can maximize any residual vision. Rehabilitation makes it possible to do things without benefit of sight. White canes and dog guides are used as mobility devices that enable blind persons to get around. And, of course, there are various forms of psychotherapy aimed at facilitating an understanding and acceptance of blindness. All of this, together with the human spirit and privileging of personhood, allows blind persons to master blindness through overcoming—that is, to live *with* blindness.

LIVING IN BLINDNESS

Living *in* blindness poses a contrasting interpretation of the relation between nature and society by preserving the distinction between the two without separating them. The "in" and the "with" are intended to represent linguistically the difference between dichotomizing nature and society (the with) and not doing so (the in). Living *in* blindness is an attempt to imagine an alternative to blindness as happenstance.

Happenstance or conditionality is indeed an essential feature of human life. Things do happen to us, beginning with the conditions prevailing at the time and place of our birth. But the interpretation of such conditions represents our need to conceive of the condition Arendt (1958) calls "human." The nature/society distinction is one way to envision the human condition. The Enlightenment recommends living *with* this distinction through the belief that society can master nature. In contrast, living *in* the nature/society distinction imagines it as a discourse. For example, the human understanding of animals is, as Berger suggested, "born of our relation with them" and this relation is born of public discourse about the nature/society distinction. We are distinguishable from nature by virtue of being *in* the midst of this public discourse.

The idea of "many natures" (MacNaughten and Urry 1995, 207) is born of this discourse. But the "pure nature," which these authors reject in favor of these socially constructed "many natures," remains firmly grounded, if not pure, in the nature/society distinction, for without it the social construction of "many natures" would be impossible. The nature/society distinction is the material out of which these many natures are socially constructed.

Social constructionism, however, marks the beginning of the recognition of the nature/society discourse and represents the first step toward a life *in* this discourse. Through the constructionist approach, we can begin to recognize that blindness is not sheerly an objective "natural fact." We see that blindness, like nature itself, is a socially constructed phenomenon that actually produces "many blindnesses." Despite their construction, however, we must still develop a relation to them and must do so in public discourse. We choose one version of blindness over another and insofar as we do so over and over again, the discourse of blindness takes on a moral character. The conception of blindness as a physical condition which can be overcome through the privileging of personhood, a conception held by the disciplines of medicine and rehabilitation, is thus not amoral. Language such as "physical condition," "adjustment," and "rehabilitation," conceal a moral conception of blindness and, to borrow from Matthews (1996), represent the "moral regulation of nature."

Living *in* blindness is to live with the awareness of being in the midst of the moral public discourse of the nature/society distinction. Blindness can remind us of this distinction and of its human origin. Sight loss puts us in mind of the natural way we once saw. It puts us in mind of the naturalness of our bodies and their vulnerability. We feel blindness, think of it, and experience it in an exclusively human way. That blindness has a natural side is a distinctly human depiction. Whatever nature has to say about itself, it says through the mouthpiece of humanity. Since humanity speaks with many voices, there are many natures. "Living with blindness" is one such voice and one such nature. It expresses the nature/humanity distinction in terms of the necessity of "the-living-with." Nature controls the conditions of life, but humanity controls *how* these conditions are lived with. Disrespect for this distinction results in an imbalance of control. The human attempt to control nature has resulted in widespread environmental destruction and the extinction and near extinction of many natural species.

The phenomenon of human blindness brings this particular nature/humanity distinction to the fore. It reminds us that nature is in control of the natural conditions of life. As Levin says, vision is a "gift from nature," and as such it may be freely given—or not. When it is not, or when the gift is taken back, we are forcefully reminded of nature's control. Nature gives or revokes vision without regard for our individual interests, purposes, hopes, and fears.

"Living with blindness" is a human response to nature as a distinct entity and as a bearer of gifts. If the gift of vision is withheld or revoked, human society attempts to remedy this anomaly through the unnatural means of medical treatment. If treatment fails, an individual will live without the gift of vision. Living *with* blindness is living *without* vision.

Living *in* blindness, however, requires a different understanding, one that goes beyond coping with and adjusting to blindness. It requires keeping blindness *alive in one's self.* Living *with* blindness raises and immediately solves the problem of blindness by conceiving of it as a condition requiring personal adjustment. Its character is unconditional and unchangeable: There is one blindness and one blindness only.

Living *in* blindness allows for the possibility of many blindnesses. Blindness can be interpreted as a dynamic rather than a static phenomenon, and this interpretation flows directly from lived experience. At times, blindness is experienced as an unalterable negative condition. At other times, it is experienced as secondary to personhood. At still other times, it is experienced as a tragedy, a stroke of unfairness, payment for wrong doings, or the bad luck of the draw. But it is also experienced as an occasion for thought. Thinking about blindness permits a blind person to live in the midst of many blindnesses and to claim blindness *as his or her own.*

Thus blindness and humanity belong together in the same way that nature and society do. The nature of blindness as well as the nature of nature are determined by the exclusively human act of interpretation. The existence of many blindnessess and many natures is as natural as the distinction between nature and humanity. As natural as this distinction is, however, we develop a relationship to it that results in the appearance of many blindnesses and many natures.

Conceiving of blindness as though it were a one-dimensional brute fact of physical nature is to abdicate any responsibility for its appearance in the world. This conception results in living *with* blindness in the same way that abdicating responsibility for nature results in living *with* it. We put up with it, we try to master it, we do what we can to adjust to and work around it.

The modern tendency is to attempt to master blindness through adaptive techniques. This approach allows for no other life than the life *with* blindness. Living *in* blindness, however, requires a different interpretive distinction. It requires that humanity recognize its essential responsibility for *any* relation to nature. Such a recognition opens the society/nature distinction to a horizon of possibilities.

THE TWO-IN-ONE

Through our movement in the world, alone together, I have come to understand my relationship with Smokie within the conception of the two-in-one. There is my body, my blindness, my nature, and my humanity; there is Smokie's domestication and his body, his nature. He is differentiated from nature by virtue of his domestication and he is differentiated from humanity by virtue of his nature. Smokie is also differentiated from many of his species by virtue of his status as a dog guide. I am differentiated from my society by virtue of my individuality; and, like Smokie, I am also differentiated from many of my species by virtue of my blindness.

Smokie and I are different from most of our respective species by virtue of our togetherness as a dog guide team. Smokie and I live *in* this differentiation. We are alone-together in two ways: We are together in our movement as one and thus alone in the social world, and we are alone by virtue of our belonging to two distinct species, as expressed in the togetherness of the nature/humanity distinction. Thus we are two in the oneness of our togetherness.

This interpretation of the differentiation in the nature/ humanity distinction moves the possibility of the relation between nature and humanity beyond the interpretive category of "mastery." Mastery requires that the nature/ humanity distinction be interpreted within the "side-by-side." Nature and humanity exist side by side each other, which allows for the possibility of one mastering the other. When humanity is conceived in terms of "mind" and nature in terms of "mindless," it is "natural" for humanity to master nature. Mastery allows nature to be handled and even *owned* by humanity. Nature may be a difficult thing to master and handle, but it is easy to own. We own our bodies, nations own rights to natural resources, and we even own our pets. The best that nature can hope for in this side-by-side relationship is that humanity will be a kind and gentle master.

The two-in-one relation between nature and humanity includes other possibilities. It can be said that I "own" Smokie only in the most technical sense. Someone owns him only insofar as the conventions of our society allow the possibility that one creature can "own" another as property. That I am his master or that I handle him are things that can be said only within the conventional side-by-side nature/humanity relationship.

What there is to be mastered, handled, or owned derives from Smokie and me—alone together. At times, we conceive of our togetherness in terms of mastering and handling the social world. We get through it, one as blind, the other as dog. We own blindness insofar as we treat it as *belonging* to us. This is one of the possibilities of the two-in-one.

The other and more interesting possibility, however, springs from *our coming in touch with our world*. For this, the ideas of mastery, handling, and ownership are insufficient forms of our relationship. At best, they take on a fluidity that the side-by-side relationship does not permit.

At one time, I am master; at another, Smokie is. Now I am handler, now he is. On one occasion, I take owner-ship for decision-making; on another, Smokie does. Re-call that Smokie and I both lead and follow one another. This is a fluid relation that does not apply when leader and follower are understood as static and completely separable entities. Thus mastery, handling, and owner-ship are situated phenomena and not ontological ones. Our situation originates in our commitment to being in touch with our world.

As we move through our world, Smokie and I are not merely side by side. We move together as one, touching and imagining both each other and our world. Our har-mony comes from the contrapuntal relation of the two-in-one interpretation of the nature/humanity distinc-tion. We depict a world to each other generated by our difference and sameness. We communicate this world to one another through the ineffability of the togetherness found in this distinction.

In her discussion of the two-in-one, Arendt (1971, 183) writes "I am not only for others but for myself, and in this latter case, I clearly am not just one. A difference is in-serted into my Oneness." As a blind person, I exist in the midst of "many blindnesses," which are expressed in the multitude of opinions and collective representations my society has of blindness. I am grist for this opinion mill. I receive opinions about blindness from professionals such as ophthalmologists and rehabilitators. My friends and acquaintances give me their opinions. Strangers comment about my blindness as Smokie and I move through the world. The mass media contribute to collec-tive representations. I am certainly for others and clearly not just one.

This multitude of opinion is not restricted to those who are sighted. Blind people have opinions about blindness too. Nor are these opinions generated strictly because they exist in distinction to sight. They exist "not because it has a relation to something else which is different . . . but because it exists among a plurality of Ideas" (Arendt, 1971, 184). Opinions about blindness are not themselves blindness. Its relationship to sight notwithstanding, blindness does not rely on sight for its existence. Blindness is only one of the many things that a society and its people have ideas about. It is only one idea among a plurality of ideas.

It is in the midst of this plurality that I, and all other blind persons, live. Privileging one version of blindness over another does not destroy or escape this plurality. The fact that the modern age conceives of blindness as a physical condition does not mean that blindness cannot be seen otherwise. Blindness as a physical condition is only one of many possible interpretations.

As Smokie and I move through our world, we are constantly in the midst of what others think of blindness. Whether we actually speak to them or not, we do respond to what they think. Our very presence to otherness is always-already a kind of response. Others make sense of us in relation to what they already think of blindness. In this sense, I *am* for others. But, as Arendt says, I am also for myself, the one who is blind. But my "one" self too is filled with the plurality of possible blindnesses. The essential difference of my society is inserted, as Arendt suggests, into my "Oneness."

Recognizing, sorting out, and judging the value of all the possible blindnesses that exist requires the kind of thought that Socrates (Theaetetus) described as a dialogue with one's self. A kind of solitude is required that Arendt (1971, 185) described as "that human situation in which I keep myself company." This kind of thinking is what Arendt called the "two-in-one."

Smokie and I move through our world *alone together*, focusing on one another in the midst of the plurality of our world and its many blindnesses. Smokie keeps me company in this estranged familiarity of opinion. I experience my blindness *together* with Smokie in this plurality. My focus is on Smokie and on myself. The world we generate springs from our communication in the midst of the world and from our movement through it.

Smokie is the essential difference "inserted into my Oneness." Who we are together comes from the dialogue between our difference and our sameness. Smokie and I are clearly the "two-in-one." Through our two-in-one Smokie gives me the opportunity to "keep myself company" with thinking about my blindness, its meaning, its various interpretations, and the horizon of possibilities it offers. My life with Smokie has shown me the need to think about blindness and to understand my responsibility for the way blindness appears in the world.

If "you want to think, you must see to it that the two who carry on the dialogue be in good shape, that the partners be *friends*" (Arendt, 1971, 187–188). From the beginning, Smokie demonstrated nothing but his desire to become my friend. He is my partner and the trust, respect, and admiration we have for one another is captured even more in the idea of friendship than in that of a bond. Despite my blindness, Smokie desired this friendship, and this taught me that my blindness is an occasion to be a decisive actor in the world. More than this, however, Smokie's friendship has taught me that I can begin to befriend my blindness and to allow it to keep me company. I am alone together with Smokie but in solitude with my blindness.

Smokie has reminded me, too, of the value of intimacy. Relationships, even the one between nature and society, are deepened and sustained through intimacy. Sometimes we control and dominate nature; at other times we are controlled and dominated by it. Without intimacy, relations between nature and society become a mere matter of dominance and submission in which "society" dominates and "nature" submits. Intimacy allows the relationship between dominance and submission to become reciprocal, fluid, and dialectical. This is what my life with Smokie has taught me. With his guidance, I have become intimate with him, with my world, and with my blindness.

Epilogue

J UST OVER a year has passed since the writing of this
book. Smokie's eighth birthday is rapidly approaching and we have been together now for over five and
a half years. We have continued our life and work together and have grown even closer over this last year. We
have experienced many changes, some more noteworthy
than others.

The most radical of these has been our relocation to
another part of Canada. In the summer of 1997, we
moved from Toronto to Antigonish, Nova Scotia. Tanya,
Cassis, Jessie, Sugar, Smokie and I left Canada's largest
city, population over two million, and took up residence
in a town of just over 5,000. We moved from a large and
diverse metropolis in Ontario to a small, largely Scottish university town on Canada's east coast. This was a
change!

Moving is one thing but moving with four animals is quite another. Add to this that, partly due to her dyslexia and partly because of the excellent public transit system in Toronto, Tanya has never learned to drive. This placed a serious limit on our transportation options. Since driving was out, our only option, or so we thought, was to fly. Tanya and I were not thrilled by this prospect. We were not concerned about Smokie, as he and I had travelled extensively by air, but Cassis, Jessie, and Sugar had never flown before. The prospect of Cassis in an airplane did not worry Tanya and me too much. Tanya had trained Cassis to work in harness and they did very well together. We felt certain that Tanya and Cassis could pass as a dog guide team and join Smokie and me in the cabin. The four of us had travelled this way by train. We had also frequented many restaurants, cafés, and other public buildings as two dog guide teams, so our concern about Cassis was minimal.

Our only concern about Cassis was her one great weakness: food. Even though Tanya has trained her to perform all other aspects of dog guide work, Cassis has great difficulty resisting food, even while in harness. Smokie will never eat while in harness and will almost never attend to any scraps of food on the street, but Cassis is another story. Tanya must be ever vigilant lest Cassis stop guiding in order to have a snack, and there was a distinct possibility that Cassis would show her true colors at meal time during the flight. Still, Tanya and I thought we could deal with this.

Our primary concern was for our two cats, Jessie and Sugar. We knew they would not be allowed to travel in the cabin but would have to travel in the baggage compartment of the plane, and we knew that they would have to be drugged for this experience. Jessie and Sugar had never been drugged before and we were anxious about how they would respond.

There was another complication. There are no direct flights from Toronto to Antigonish. We would have to fly from Toronto to Halifax, a two-hour flight. From there we would have to take a bus to Antigonish, at least another three hours. Factoring in travel time to and from airports and bus stations, Tanya and I anticipated a seven- to eight-hour journey. The prospect was less than appealing. As Tanya and I planned the trip, the hope that "Well, we'll do it . . . somehow," became a frequent refrain.

About a month before we were to leave Toronto, Tanya, Cassis, Smokie, and I were sitting in our favorite neighborhood bar talking about our upcoming "crazy trip" with two friends, Gord and Ron. There was much teasing, laughter, and speculation as to how many meal trays Cassis would manage to snatch during the flight. Our friends knew that Tanya and I were very concerned about this trip and were doing their best to quell our anxiety with humor.

Then, in the most sober and serious way possible, Gord asked, "What about the van? Why not rent the van like you were thinking before?" Earlier that year, when Tanya completed her Ph.D. in sociology, we had seriously considered moving to a smaller city only a two-hour drive from Toronto, where a university teaching job for Tanya seemed imminent. Gord had agreed to drive us. We would rent a van, load everyone into it, and drive the two hours to our new home. But, as is often the case in academia nowadays, Tanya's job fell through. When Tanya later accepted a position at St. Francis Xavier University in Antigonish, almost a third of the way across Canada from Toronto, we assumed our "van plan" was out.

Ron, who is from Halifax, picked up on the van idea immediately. We pulled out calendars, consulted work schedules, set dates and times—in a few minutes, our travel plans were made, and we resumed our laughing and good times. The very next day we confirmed plans and I arranged for the rental of a van. In three weeks, Gord and Ron would be driving us to our new home. We calculated that the trip would take approximately two and a half days. Gord and Ron would drop us off in Antigonish and proceed to Halifax for a couple of days, then return to Antigonish, say their goodbyes, and drive the van back to Toronto.

All of this seemed quite simple, and it was until we were on our way. Early in the evening of our departure day, we loaded the van with our suitcases, some books and papers, and a few other things we would need before the rest of our belongings arrived in Antigonish a few weeks later. Then the live cargo—two dogs, two cats, two cat crates, a litter box, water, food, and, oh yes, three sighties and a blind guy—all in the van, safe and secure and off to Antigonish. I had two harnesses for Smokie in the event that one might break. Cassis's harness was stowed safely in the van. Half an hour later we were reaching the outskirts of Toronto on our way east, when I remembered Smokie's leash! I had forgotten both his leash and collar. Back we went. About an hour later, we were at the outskirts of Toronto making our way east . . . once again.

The most interesting part of the trip, other than the spectacle of the "zoo on wheels," was checking into hotels and eating in restaurants. Despite our organizational meeting at the bar, or perhaps because of it, we had not thought to arrange to stay in hotels that allowed pets. Smokie, of course, was not a problem in this regard, but the other three animals were. Smokie, Gord, and I did the checking in. We secured a room for Gord and Ron and one for Tanya and me and the others. Gord, Smokie, and I then returned to the van, where the adventure began. The trick was to sneak Jessie and Sugar (along with their food and litter box) into the hotel room without being seen. We were fortunate on both nightly stopovers that we were able to park the van near an entrance that did not take us through the lobby.

Sneaking Cassis in was not necessary. Tanya had trained Cassis in the fundamentals of guide work and she guided Tanya quite competently. Cassis looked like a real dog guide and in a sense she was. The only thing that stands between Cassis and real dog guide status is that Tanya is not a real blind person.

Getting Jessie and Sugar into the hotel room, though tricky, was not too big an adventure. Convincing hotel staff that Cassis was a real dog guide with a legal right to be in the hotel presented a problem, however. In her harness, Cassis looked like a real dog guide; the trouble was that she was guiding a sighted person. The trick now was for Tanya to look like a real blind person.

The first night things went smoothly enough. We arrived at the hotel shortly before midnight. Gord, Smokie, and I checked in and I explained to the desk clerk that Smokie was my dog guide and that my partner, Tanya, also used one. We were able to park the van near an entrance that led directly to our rooms and it was not necessary to enter the lobby. Apart from some anxiety on the part of the desk clerk, who said she had never seen a dog guide before and wondered if they were classified as pets, this first night presented us with little difficulty.

The second evening we arrived at our big hotel, looking forward to enjoying its facilities and particularly its fine restaurant, which would be a welcome change from the snacks we had brought from Toronto and fast food restaurants on the road. Because we were able to park the van at an entrance that did not take us through the hotel lobby, sneaking Jessie and Sugar in was relatively easy; we only had to avoid some hotel cleaning staff. Shortly before six o'clock, we were all securely in our rooms. Tanya and I fed everyone and made sure they all had water. Then we harnessed our dog guides and proceeded around the back of the hotel and across the street to a park. Smokie and Cassis played and ran off the stiffness of the day's journey. After they had relieved themselves for the last time, the four of us returned to our room. We then telephoned Gord and Ron and arranged to meet them for dinner.

Tanya put on her sunglasses in preparation for our trip through the maze of hotel hallways, into the lobby, and through to the restaurant. They obscured her eyes somewhat but did not hide them completely, so she stood in front of the bathroom mirror and practiced not making eye contact. This proved to be more difficult than Tanya had expected. In one sense, she had no difficulty in not making eye contact; she could, after all, look directly away from the mirror. But Tanya soon discovered that there was more to "not making eye contact" than making no contact at all. Tanya had been with me on many occasions when people complimented me on my ability to make eye contact even though I could not see them, and she knew that I did this only occasionally, since constant eye contact could lead people to wonder whether or not I was blind.

Tanya first practiced coming close to eye contact, thus giving people the impression that she was a blind person who knew the ropes of the sighted world. This mastered, she practiced occasional direct eye contact, as if she were a blind person who was good at this sort of "sightie stuff." Tanya had spent a considerable amount of time working Cassis in harness on the streets of Toronto, but she had never entered a restaurant with her. After approximately twenty minutes of practice, Tanya and her dog guide were ready.

As we opened the door and stepped out into the hallway, I could feel the tension. We stood side by side, dog guide team alongside dog guide team. I turned my head slowly toward Tanya, being careful not to make direct eye contact, and in an expectant voice said, "Ready?" Not directly returning my look, Tanya took a deep breath and said "Ready." The words "forward Smokie" and "forward Cassis" came simultaneously and we were on our way.

The dogs worked very well. They guided us quickly and confidently through the twists and turns of the hallways. A sudden change of floor covering and a more echoing sensation told me we had entered the lobby. I asked Smokie to stay and Tanya did the same to Cassis. People milled about in the lobby. The entrance to the restaurant loomed ahead, directly across the lobby from where we were standing. My fingers gently flexed on Smokie's harness. Tanya cleared her throat. Once more, the simultaneous commands "forward Smokie, forward Cassis." The dogs sensed the seriousness of what they were about to do. Their muscular shoulders moved forward in their harnesses and they stepped confidently and gracefully into the lobby.

Unfortunately, Tanya's first step was not as graceful. She stumbled slightly on the edge of the carpeting separating the hallway from the lobby, which caused Cassis to think Tanya was in trouble. She spun and quickly put her front paws on Tanya's legs. Looking directly at her, Tanya told Cassis that everything was okay, and dog guide and blind person returned to their walking position. Meanwhile, I had asked Smokie to stay while we waited for our partners to regroup. Our second attempt managed to embody the grace of dog guide movement. We moved quickly through the lobby and stopped just inside the restaurant. A few moments later, Gord and Ron joined us and a maitre d' showed us to a table in one of the restaurant's many rooms which, except for us, was unoccupied.

Smokie and, surprisingly, Cassis lay at our feet and were well behaved during the entire meal. Tanya did very well at not making eye contact with the waiter. As he did for me, the waiter explained where things were to Tanya. He told her where he was placing her drink, where her silverware was, and always warned her when he was bringing something to her. She definitely looked blind, in spite of Gord's attempts to trick her into seeing. As the waiter approached, Gord would say, "Tanya, pass me the butter." Only once did Tanya's hand move toward the butter, but she quickly recovered by feigning to explore the objects on the table. Blind as she was, Tanya was also able to get through the process of taking care of the bill by using her credit card.

The relaxing dinner over, we left the restaurant as gracefully as we had entered. Across the lobby, through the front doors and across the street, Tanya and I, with our dog guides, found the entrance of the small park. We removed the harnesses and leashes from our guides and let them have their turn at relaxing.

OUR NEW HOME

At about two o'clock the next day, the "zoo on wheels" entered the town of Antigonish. We all felt a sense of relief, Tanya and I because our long ride in the back of a van with four animals was over, and Gord and Ron because their long drive, with all the chaos of life in the van, was over. The van buzzed with excitement; we were in our new hometown. The short drive through the town to the university was accompanied by cheerful sardonic descriptions of the town by Gord and Ron and by Tanya's excitement.

> Gord: Hey, there's a barber shop. It's a real barber shop. You'll be in there soon, Rod, saying, 'Just a little off the sides Floyd.'
> Ron: Look, Main Street. Geez, there must be almost, well, geez, almost three people on it.
> Tanya: It's gorgeous Rod. The town is really pretty.
> Gord: Man, it's gonna to take Smokie . . . I bet it'll take him, god, almost three and a half minutes to learn this town.
> Ron: You think? I bet it takes him only three.
> Tanya: Wow! Fields, bushes—they can run forever here.

Though the town was small, the university was not. Once we had reached it, we needed to locate the security office. Tanya and I had arranged to live temporarily in a university residence apartment while we searched for permanent housing. We secured the key and drove on to our small but comfortably furnished two-bedroom apartment, which was surrounded by acres of lawns and woods. Leaving Gord and Ron behind in the apartment to enjoy a well-deserved beer, Tanya and I explored the surroundings with Smokie and Cassis. Their excitement and noses took them everywhere. Tanya and I followed them as they ran across the lawns and through the bushes. Given his love of water, it was no surprise to us that Smokie discovered a swamp. About forty-five minutes later, Tanya and I returned to the apartment with two tired, slightly dirty, but very happy dogs.

Ron drove Tanya to a supermarket, where she picked up groceries and other things we would need. This done, Gord and Ron were off to Halifax. They would be returning to Antigonish in two days to spend the evening with us before heading back to Toronto.

The next two days proved hectic and somewhat frightening for Tanya and me. Finding a house to rent for the six of us turned out to be a very difficult task. Antigonish is a small town and four thousand students descend on it at the beginning of the university year. There were very few houses to rent, and it seemed that everyone who had a house for rent rented it "by the room" to students. Rents in Antigonish, we were surprised to learn, were as high as those in Toronto.

By the time Gord and Ron returned, Tanya and I were a little disappointed and wondering whether we had done the right thing in moving. Despite our doubts, the four of us, along with our two dog guides, spent an enjoyable evening in a local bar. Amidst all the joking about Antigonish, Gord and Ron kindly permitted Tanya and me to vent our frustrations. They also helped us to put things into perspective.

Saying goodbye the next morning was an emotional moment for all of us. Gord and Ron slowly made their way to the van. Assuming the residence apartment was just another hotel stop, Smokie and Cassis did the same. We finally convinced them that they were staying, and a few moments later the four of us stood quietly watching as the van disappeared. Smokie sat by my side and gently leaned against my knee, somehow knowing, it seemed to me, that we would not be seeing our friends for a very long time. Making our new home would now begin in earnest.

LIFE ON THE STREETS

We spent the next several weeks looking for a house to rent. Since neither one of us drives, we had to find a house within walking distance of the university. Scores of phone calls yielded only three possibilities, and each one was very small, very expensive, and totally unsuited to our needs. A month later, we were desperate and began looking for apartments, which proved just as difficult. Finally the culture of a small town, which had made it so difficult for us to find a house, paid off. "Word of mouth" found us a very large house with a huge yard near the university and, most important to Smokie and Cassis, near a large field, woods, and a stream. Tanya and I immediately signed a lease and prepared to take occupancy in three weeks. At last we were able to relax. Smokie and Cassis were enjoying the acres of land around the apartment and we began to explore our new town without the worry of finding a new home.

For Smokie and me, the most interesting thing about exploring our new town was that we did it with Tanya and Cassis. With both dogs in harness, we found the veterinarian and post office, transferred accounts at the bank, shopped at the supermarket, ate at restaurants, and enjoyed the breaks we took at what soon became our very friendly local bar. No matter where we went, everyone wanted to know about the dog guides. No one, anywhere, refused us entry into a public establishment. This had not been the case in Toronto. We were enjoying our new home very much.

The four of us were certainly a spectacle on the streets of Antigonish. Smokie's customary speed always put us in the lead, a few seconds ahead of Tanya and Cassis, and it did not take long to get the lay of the land. Not only did we quickly become familiar with the streets of Antigonish, we also became familiar with its Scottish culture. The four of us attended ceilidhs and other Scottish musical events, and Tanya and I discovered that both Smokie and Cassis enjoyed the bagpipes. When they hear bagpipes as they sit beside us—and they hear them very often in Antigonish—Smokie and Cassis lie down, relax, and go to sleep.

Although Tanya was enjoying working Cassis in harness, she had never worked so much before, and although the people of Antigonish were very friendly, the small-town character of the place presented Tanya with a problem she had never experienced in Toronto. The people in our Toronto neighborhood knew Tanya and Cassis and knew that Tanya had trained Cassis to do dog guide work. People would often see the four of us walking down the street together. But the people in our Toronto neighborhood also knew that Tanya was not blind. When people in Antigonish see Tanya and Cassis, however, they see a blind person being guided by a dog guide. The anonymity of a big city had prevented Tanya from experiencing this as a problem, but the small-town character of Antigonish brought Tanya face to face with the problematic nature of this experience. On the rare occasions when the four of us had ventured into unfamiliar parts of Toronto, Tanya had been able to "act blind"; the problem she now faced in Antigonish was somewhat different but no easier to solve.

During our first week in Antigonish, Tanya and I, together with our guides, had been to many places. When we entered the bank for the first time, a staff person greeted us, "So you're the new blind couple in town. Welcome to Antigonish. How may I help you?" Tanya quickly explained, "No, I'm just training her. I'm sighted. He's the real dog guide and he's the real blind person." Tanya soon realized that unless she did something about it, she would be seen and known as a blind person in Antigonish. In itself, this was not problematic for Tanya. But since she would be living in Antigonish, shopping in the town, going to the bank, and teaching at the university—and doing all this for the most part without Cassis—being seen and known as a blind person soon became a problem.

Tanya had perfected her ability to act blind, but now she had to act sighted. This proved just as difficult and as fraught with anxiety for Tanya as her earlier experiences acting blind had been. The irony of the situation was rich. Tanya soon made and attached a sign to Cassis's harness that read "dog guide in training."

I too experienced a problem in Antigonish that I had not experienced in Toronto. Smokie had found "rest stops" in Toronto, small areas of grass and trees scattered here and there among the miles of streets and sidewalks. As he came upon one of these rare rest stops, Smokie would lead me from the sidewalk and onto the grass, whereupon I would remove his harness and he would "rest" in the way dogs do, wandering around, peeing and sniffing. After a few minutes of this resting, I would harness Smokie up and we would be on our way. In our new environment, rest stops abound; the streets and sidewalks of Antigonish are scattered here and there among the miles of grass and trees. The frequency of Smokie's rest stops has increased dramatically and he spends much more time resting now.

ARRIVING BLIND

I am not a stranger to the many regions of Canada. I was born in Saskatchewan and spent my early childhood in a small prairie town. My family then moved to Winnipeg, and until early adulthood I lived in that city's infamous North End. For several years after that, I lived in Vancouver while attending graduate school. After spending a few years in Toronto, I taught sociology in Alberta for several years and returned to Toronto for a few more years. But this most recent move to Nova Scotia is unique; it is the first time I have arrived in a new place *this blind*. Everywhere else I have ever lived, my eyesight was at the top end of the legally blind scale and in the country of the legally blind, this is "good sight." Becoming oriented to these locations and learning to "get around" in them proved relatively easy. My residual vision made it possible for me to rely, at least to some degree, upon sight as a means of orientation.

When I lost most of my residual vision approximately five years ago, I was living in a familiar city. Though Smokie showed me parts of Toronto I had never experienced before, I was very familiar with the general layout and geography of that city. Moving to Antigonish was a completely different story. Although I travelled extensively in Atlantic Canada years ago, I had not spent any time in Antigonish and did not know it at all. I arrived there blind, and for the first time in my life vision played absolutely no role in becoming oriented to new surroundings.

This situation weighed anxiously on me for several weeks before our move. I spoke extensively with Tanya about it and even mentioned it to a few close friends. I was not so much looking for a solution to a problem as I was seeking to express my anxiety, which swept the memories of my childhood through my mind and guided me back to the early days when I experienced my first significant loss of sight.

I was not especially concerned with my ability to get around Antigonish safely; after all, I had Smokie. Getting hit by a car, smacking into a telephone post, falling down a flight of stairs—these things were not my concern. Smokie and I had made our way through the streets of many unfamiliar towns and cities. But those were short business trips, lasting a few days at most. Moving to Antigonish was a different thing altogether. When Smokie and I arrived home in Toronto almost five years ago, our identity as a dog guide team took time to form. Previously, most people had assumed I was either sighted or else had some mild vision impairment; suddenly, with

Smokie at my side, everyone knew I was blind. Smokie and I shaped my new identity together, but I had the advantage in Toronto that people already knew me. They had to adjust to my blindness, but they already knew *me* apart from my blindness.

We arrived in Antigonish, however, as complete strangers. My arrival with Smokie would tell the people of the town *what* I was but not *who* I was. From my very first step in my new home, my identity would take shape on the basis of how the people of Antigonish conceived of blindness and how I exemplified it. I arrived in Antigonish wearing my blindness in a way I had never worn it before.

Would I be able to orient myself to the geographical layout of Antigonish as a home? What conceptions of blindness would I encounter in Antigonish? Would I be able to figure the place out? Who would I be in Antigonish?

These anxieties were complicated by the smallness of Antigonish. Unlike Toronto, where encounters with strangers never to be met again were a daily occurrence, encounters with people on the streets of Antigonish would be "forever." It is often said of small places that the "town talks" (Bonner, 1997), and Smokie and I were sure to be grist for the mill. It did not take long for this to happen. Soon after arriving in Antigonish, I had lunch at one of the local cafés. Upon entering, Smokie and I were given a very friendly welcome and were shown to a table. The waitress said, "I see you two walking by here all the time. My friend Maggie at the bank told me all about you two."

Thus I arrived in my new home, a small town where everyone knew everyone else's business, blinder than I had ever been.

ADJUSTMENTS ON THE STREET

Only six weeks have passed since our arrival in Antigonish. We have come to know some people, have become acquainted with many more, and have spoken with everyone in the town, or so it seems. Because our new home "talks," Smokie and I have had to make a few adjustments to the ways in which we typically conduct our life "on the street."

Smokie and I have always noticed that we were being noticed, but now we also notice that our being noticed is also being remembered and talked about. We have always known that our reputation precedes us. No matter where we went in Toronto, our reputation as blind person and dog guide went before us, serving as a building block in the construction of our identity. Our reputation walks ahead of us in Antigonish, too, but it walks hand in hand with our identity. We move through the streets of Antigonish not only as blind person and dog guide but also as Rod and Smokie.

I have had to make an adjustment in the way I talk with Smokie as we move through Antigonish. I always speak to Smokie as we work, communicating back to him the "rush" he gives me in his graceful, fluid movements, stopping, starting, weaving, and duking his way down a busy street. I praise him as though he were an athlete; I say "good move Smoke, good job" and a lot of enthusiastic "yeses." When Smokie avoids a swerving car or bicycle, my praise is even more enthusiastic. I immediately ask him to find a wall of a building or some other "safe place," where I remove his harness and the celebration begins. I praise him, he jumps on me, I give him a treat, and after harnessing him up again we are on our way. The rush I experience from working Smokie expresses itself in a constant flow of enthusiasm.

Smokie's athletic possibilities have suffered somewhat in Antigonish. Compared to Toronto, the streets of Antigonish are almost empty; there are very few pedestrians, almost no other obstacles, construction sites are almost non-existent, and swerving cars and bicycles are extremely rare. My enthusiasm has not waned, but I am now praising Smokie for such mundane things as stopping at curbs. Still, I am very much missing our athletics.

Not only do I speak to Smokie about his "moves" while we are working, I also provide him with a running commentary of how I am experiencing people. For example, I sometimes give an uncomplimentary comment or gesture to a person in a car who has swerved in front of us or to a cyclist who has come close to hitting us. This is just how it is in a big city; it is expected. My chances of running into the person I have just yelled at, let alone the chances that we know each other, are almost nil. Not so in Antigonish. In fact, the chances of my *not* running into that person again are nil. Thus, my second adjustment— my yelling and gesturing are as rare in Antigonish as construction sites.

The third adjustment concerns the comments I used to make about certain "types" of people we encountered in the various neighborhoods of Toronto. Smokie and I often walked through an area of Toronto known as Yorkville, an old neighborhood that was home to many members of the hippie movement in the 1960s. Since then, Yorkville has been renovated and gentrified with exclusive shops and restaurants, and Smokie used to receive many compliments as we walked through the area. "What a gorgeous dog," we would hear, and "Oh, he is so sweet," "What a cute dog!" I often responded, "They're just yuppies, Smoke, ignore them." For the same reason that I no longer yell or gesture, I have dropped the use of such comments in Antigonish.

I have also eliminated the "tall tales" about how Smokie can distinguish traffic lights and read addresses. If I tell one person in Antigonish that Smokie can read numbers, I have told everyone. While everyone has conceptions of Smokie's reputation as a dog guide, not everyone is susceptible to believing exaggerated accounts of his intelligence. I am minimizing the possibility of the clerk at the drug store or the waitress at the pub saying, "So now Smokie can read numbers." I still joke with people about Smokie's supernatural abilities, but I make clear that I am joking.

I have made one final adjustment in Antigonish. Because of the town's size, very little here challenges Smokie. Remember, Smokie likes to work hard, and without challenges and new adventures, he may get bored. I have worried about this, and I have tried to come up with activities and adventures that will engage him more fully. One challenge I have presented to Smokie over the past few weeks is the taking of short cuts. He has been trained to "square up" at curbs, never cut corners, and always stay on the sidewalk. On those occasions when Smokie *must* lead me off the sidewalk and onto the street, as when we need to detour around a construction site, he will take me to the curb, proceed quickly around the construction site, and go back to the curb and up onto the sidewalk again. All of this precision is not engaged in merely for its own sake; it is necessary in order for me to remain oriented to my surroundings. Cutting corners when turning from one sidewalk onto another, for example, could disorient me. Coming directly up to an intersecting curb and then turning onto another sidewalk allows me to keep track of exactly where I am. For these reasons, Smokie has never taken short cuts.

In Antigonish, I thought that learning how to take "short cuts" would be an interesting challenge for us both. We began our lessons on the university campus, some thirty buildings, several football fields, and tennis courts, all situated on several acres of treed lawns connected by a maze of sidewalks and streets.

After a few days of familiarizing ourselves with the university, our "short cut" challenge began. The idea for such a challenge actually came from Smokie. We had spent much time on the university campus over the course of several days. On one of our trips, Smokie took me off the sidewalk. I assumed it was one of his "rest stops," until he did not stop as usual. He proceeded approximately thirty feet across a lawn to a connecting sidewalk. He took his first short cut. After that, I began calling each sidewalk a "curb." For example, I would ask Smokie to go "right" and leave the sidewalk. I would then ask him to "find a curb," and he would find another sidewalk. A few days of this and Smokie was taking short cuts all over the campus. I am sometimes disoriented, but he is not. No matter where we are on the campus, I need merely say, "let's go home, Smokie" and, short cuts and all, he leads me off the campus and home.

These are the only adjustments Smokie and I have made since arriving in Antigonish six weeks ago. I am certain that we will make more. I have not yet, for example, been asked "Do you know where you're going?" or "Do you know where you are?" I am quite sure that these questions will come and I am just as sure that I will make some adjustment to my usual responses.

"Arriving blind" in a new home was the most significant aspect of the move for me. I knew that everyone would see and come to know me as blind. I would not be explaining that I was "legally blind" but that I could see enough "to get around." I knew that there would be nothing to explain to people in Antigonish. When they saw Smokie and his harness, they would "see" that I was blind.

As he did in Toronto, Smokie would "release" my blindness into Antigonish. I "walked into blindness" with Smokie in Toronto and I knew that he would walk me into my blindness in Antigonish with the same disregard for anyone's conception of blindness that he did in Toronto. He did not disappoint me.

Once again, Smokie walked me into blindness with an enthusiasm and pride which spilled over into me. Contributing to this was the fact that Tanya and her "dog guide," Cassis, often accompanied us on this walk. On these occasions, I felt my blindness being released by two canine partners and one human one. I thought that "walking into blindness" was the greatest "gift of vision" I could ever have received, and so I was not expecting an even greater one. But as we walk into blindness through the streets of Antigonish I am accompanied on a walk I have never taken before—a "walk with blindness."

Notes

Chapter 2

1. Smith (1987, 47) writes, "'A sociology for women' traces the site of women's emerging consciousness in the gender subtext of the relations of ruling, which I have outlined in the Introduction, and proposes a strategy of inquiry I have called 'the everyday world as problematic,' that is, an organization of inquiry that begins with where women *actually* are and addresses the problem of how our everyday worlds are put together in relations that are not wholly discoverable within the everyday world." "Actual blind persons" makes reference to the everyday world in which they live and which is constructed in relation to a hegemonic version of sight. This results in a "Sociology of Marginality" wherein relations to the everyday world are discoverable through a re-conceiving of the taken-for-granted as hegemony and as reproduction of the "center." For an excellent discussion of such a sociology in relation to art, see Titchkosky (1997).

2. Thus vision remains silent and speaks only when addressed. Addressing vision requires an inquiry which recognizes the silent character of vision and the taken for granted character of the social world. "Nothing is so silent as that which is taken-for-granted and self-evident. Therefore, silence makes human research and writing both possible and necessary" (Van Manen, 1990, 12).

3. "Passing" is a phenomenon I deal with extensively elsewhere (Michalko 1998, 102ff, 1982, 9–30).

4. Some blind persons have written about their experience with dog guides. For the most part, however, these are romanticized versions of the dog guide. See, for example, Hickford (1973), Dickson (1942). There are also some historical accounts of dog guides, for example, Chevigny (1946). Ed and Toni Eames (1994) have written an excellent guide to dog guide schools in North America. The most interesting aspect of their work is that they treat blind persons as "consumers." The social sciences have recently topicalized animal/human relations. See, for example, Wieder (1980), Fogle (1988), Arluke (1988), Shapiro (1990), Sanders (1990, 1993). Research is beginning to appear in relation to "service dogs," for example, Eddy et al. (1988), Deshen and Deshen (1989), Valentine et al. (1993), Sanders (1996).

5. There has been an interesting development together with a growing body of literature in the area of the senses under the rubric of the "anthropology of the senses." See, for example, Howes (1991), Synnott (1993), Leder (1990), Classen (1993).

6. This may or may not have been empirically correct. With sight as the distance sense, it is possible that only one-half of Leo's body was in front of me. My "new" distance sense, however, told me otherwise. Empiricism relies heavily on sight as the distance sense.

7. In his work on the development of "identity," Taylor (1989, 525) writes of the necessity for a name. "My name is what I am 'called.' A human being *has* to have a name, because he or she has to be *called*, i.e., addressed. Being called into conversation is a precondition of developing a human identity, and so my name is (usually) given me by my earliest interlocutors." Working with a dog guide may be understood as a "conversation" between blind person and dog. Thus the dog must have a name if he is to be addressed and "called" into the conversation that is dog guide work.

8. I address this in detail elsewhere (Michalko 1998).

9. Arendt (1971, 19–26) speaks of the invisible in the visible, i.e., of what resides in appearances but cannot be seen with the eye. This stems from Plato's cave metaphor (*Republic,* Bk. VII).

10. Arendt (1977, 65) connects the "as if" to imagination and judgment. This is precisely what Diderot's blind man does. He imagines that longer arms would put him in touch with "what goes on" in the world and judges this gift as having a far greater value than the "natural gift of vision."

11. For an excellent analysis of the "from and to" of the phenomenal world, see Leder (1990, esp. 15–17).

12. As Ong (1991, 28) suggests, the organization of our senses is "in part determined by culture while at the same time it makes culture." I was reorganizing my senses in relation to cultural determination while at the same time coming to "understand," that is "make" my culture.

13. For a historical overview of the role of sight in Western thought, see Synnott (1991, 61–78).

14. Hall (1966, 65) writes, "The information gathered by a blind man outdoors is limited to a circle with a radius of twenty to one hundred feet. With sight, he could see the stars. The talented blind are limited to an average *maximum* speed of two to three miles an hour over familiar territory. With sight, man has to fly faster than sound before he begins to need aids to avoid bumping into things." The first mistake Hall makes is to equate the ability to see stars with information. Blind people know that stars exist and that they can be seen—they have that information. His second mistake is that he arbitrarily uses "twenty to one hundred feet" as the experiential realm of blind persons. Third, Hall "thinks" that sighted persons stumble only when moving at "MACH 1." Even with an experiential realm of twenty to one hundred feet, one notices that sighted persons stumble from time to time, even when they are not flying by at the speed of sound. The overall mistake that Hall makes is looking at blindness through the paradigm of sight. In this

segment of his work, Hall clearly exhibits the bias and hegemony of sight. Talented or not, blind persons, like their talented sighted counterparts, do stumble from time to time. Hall himself trips over blindness.

15. Sanders (1993) analyzes the attribution of "mindedness" by humans to dogs and other animals. Mindedness is an essentially human phenomenon. Attributing it to dogs suggests that they do not possess minds in the ways humans do. Sanders is suggesting that the mindedness of dogs is a phenomenon that is socially achieved through the society/nature dialectic.

Chapter 3

1. The idea that dogs have evolved from wolves and display behavior such as packing, dominance, and submission is a ubiquitous concept in most dog training enterprises. See, for example, Saunders 1954; Neville 1991; Knott 1994. However, I will focus only on the training of dog guides.

2. Scott's (1969) research represents a seminal work which demonstrates the ways in which organizations "for the blind" present images of blindness and how these organizations expect blind persons to adopt these images as part of their identity. As Scott points out (ibid., 121), "Blind men are not born, they are made." They are "made" through the images which organizations designed to help blind persons socially impose on them as a feature of that help. For an excellent analysis of the social consequences that result from various ways of conceiving of blind persons as a group in need of help, see Blum (1982, 64–82).

Chapter 4

1. Doubt (1996, 3–30) explores this Hegelian concept in his work on schizophrenia. Howes and others have addressed Hegel's idea of "sense-certainty" under the rubric of the "anthropology of the senses." As I tried to show in chapter 2, Howes's work provides for the possibility of a more inclusive analysis of touch

and sight in the study of blindness. Said's work on exiles and Hegel's concept of "sense-certainty" open the way for a clearer understanding of the "power" of the senses.

2. This process and many others are being addressed in a growing body of literature collected under the rubric of "Disability Studies." For excellent examples, see Zola (1982), Gadacz (1994), Ingstad and Reynolds Whyte (1995), and Davis (1997).

3. This is true unless blindness is seen as a direct effect of poverty or poor health caused by impoverished living conditions or as an effect of inadequate medical services.

4. For an excellent analysis of how social products and production act as a "sign" of a social order, see Baudrillard (1981).

Chapter 5

1. Following Arendt, Titchkosky (1997) develops the idea of "between-ness" as a way to make a place for marginality and marginal people in the world. She speaks of the "essential between-ness" of the dialectic movement between the margins and the center.

2. I have been influenced greatly by the work of Erving Goffman, especially his *Behavior in Public Places* (1963), in my analysis of the interaction Smokie and I experience in public.

3. Brooks Gardner (1980) analyzes "street remarks" aimed at women. These remarks are oriented first to the identity "woman" and second, to the reputation some men attach to that identity. Brooks Gardner raises the "ambiguity" such street remarks often engender. A man says to a woman crossing the street, "Hey there! I know you not lookin' at me, but you sure are one fine woman!" (ibid., 51). Brooks Gardner argues that the interpretation of such remarks, whether as complimentary or sexist, is a social construction.

4. The idea of the "first word" is an impossibility since it presupposes language. The same might be said in relation to the "first step" since it presupposes the language of mobility. The "first word" can only be heard when the child is seen through the

eyes of empiricism and heard with the ears of a correspondence understanding of language. The first word or first anything is an idealization constructed for the purposes of developing an empirical conception of the social world. This is also true for the "natural world." Despite Copernicus, as Gadamer (1988, 407) says, "the sun has not ceased to set for us."

5. When a blind person "behaves well," acts "normally," he or she is also interpreted as overcoming the "naturally negative condition" of blindness. That one blind person overcomes natural inclinations, however, does not mean that all do. Desire and will to do so are very much at play. Thus the membership category "blind person" provides an interpretive scheme for those "actual" blind persons who "adjust well" as well as for those who do not. Membership categories always include interpretive room for particularity.

6. For an excellent analysis of the development of this debate see Cornel West (1990, 19–38). West argues that this debate stems from the need of those who are conceived as "marginal" to develop their social identities. This need has given rise, according to West, to a "new cultural politics of difference." It is worth noting that while West includes in his analysis every "marginal" category he can think of, he excludes those of us who are disabled. This exclusion suggests that disability belongs more to the realm of "natural events" than to the realm of human achievement. As "natural events," disabled persons are not yet understood as a "people." As "no longer and not yet" a people, disabled persons exist "between" humanity and nature. Thus West's exclusion of disabled persons is not simply a "forgetting" but an act oriented to the essential "betweenness" of those of us who are disabled.

7. For a popular rendering of this interpretation see Morris (1969).

8. I address the difference between training and education in "The Opening of the Bureaucratic Mind: Putting Good Works

Into Practice" (1995), presented at the 1995 CIRLA conference.

9. For a detailed discussion of this process from the point of view
of dog guide trainers and breeders, see Pfaffenberger (1963)
and Hartwell (1942).

10. With regard to this issue, Pfaffenberger (1963, 159) quotes
Ginsberg: "Proper socialization, handling and training are
necessary to realize the potential that exists in even the best
strains. On the other hand, superior socialization, handling
and training will not make a good Guide Dog out of inferior
genetic stock. The successfully trained Guide Dog results of-
tener and truer from the line-bred individuals of carefully selected stock than from the out-crosses of even excellent individuals. One importance of line-breeding is to achieve uniform
results."

11. This "matching process" is discussed by Robson (1985).

12. Farley Mowat's 1963 account of his study of wolves illustrates
this point. Insofar as people and wolves live at the same time
and in the same place, they *co-habit* the world. But Mowat came
to know the individual wolves he was studying. He gave them
names, shared food with them, and so on. In this sense, he *co-
existed* with wolves in a common world. Mowat's experience em-
bodied the Inuit creation legend of the wolf.

13. I wanted a dog guide partly because I needed help and partly
because I love dogs. Regardless of my motives, I held dog
guides in the same high esteem that many people do. I was also
aware of their reputation. Part of this meant that I wanted independence but I wanted it with dignity. Many blind persons
share this conception. Sentimentality vis dog guides is sometimes secondary to this desire for dignified independence.
Blunkett (1995, 78) puts the issue this way: "It had never been
my intention to acquire a guide dog. Throughout my teens,
from time to time I had come across guide dogs or heard
people speaking about them, usually, but not exclusively, in

highly sentimental terms. I felt this presented the wrong image, and that a guide dog's work as an aid to independence,
dignity and mobility should be of more crucial importance."
Of course, dignity and independence cannot be spoken of or
even felt without sentiment.

Chapter 6

1. All dog training is steeped in this implied distinction. See, for
   example, Knott and Cooper (1994), Coode (1993), Neville
   (1991), Saunders (1978).
2. Schutz (1973, 11f) refers to this phenomenon as a "reciprocity
   of perspectives." Berger and Luckman (1966, 231) call it "reciprocal typification." These authors permit us to see, first, that
   "help" organizationally institutionalizes interaction between
   blind and sighted persons. Second, we get a clear "look" at the
   concept of "reciprocity of perspectives" in action. Persons who
   ask me "Do you know where you are going?" are saying, "If I
   were blind and in your position, *I* would need help." This type
   of question is addressed to the one who asks it more than to
   the one of whom it is asked.

Chapter 7

1. For an excellent review of research on the animal/human distinction see Wolfe (1993, 28–54).
2. I deal with this distinction somewhat differently in *The Mystery
   of the Eye and the Shadow of Blindness* (Toronto: University of Toronto Press, 1998).

Bibliography

Arendt, Hannah. *Between Past and Future: Eight Exercises in Political Thought.* Harmondsworth, Middlesex: Penguin Books, 1954.

————. *The Human Condition.* Chicago: The University of Chicago Press, 1958.

————. *The Life of the Mind: Thinking and Willing.* San Diego: Harcourt Brace Jovanovich, 1971.

————. *Lectures on Kant's Political Philosophy.* Chicago: The University of Chicago Press, 1982.

Aristotle. *Nichomacheon Ethics.* Indianapolis: Library of Liberal Arts, 1962.

Arluke, Arnold. "Sacrificial Symbolism in Animal Experimentation: Object or Pet?" *Anthrozoos.* 2 (1988): 98–117.

Barraga, Natalie. *Visual Handicaps and Learning* Houston: Exceptional Resources, 1983.

Baudrillard, Jean. *For a Critique of the Political Economy of the Sign.* U.S.A.: Telos Press, Ltd., 1981.

Berger, John. *About Looking.* New York: Pantheon Books, 1980.

Berger, Peter. *Invitation To Sociology: A Humanistic Perspective.* New York: Doubleday, 1963.

————and Thomas Luckman. *The Social Construction of Reality.* New York: Doubleday, 1966.

Blum, Alan. "Victim, Patient, Client, Pariah: Steps in the Self-Understanding of the Experience of Suffering and Affliction." *Reflections: Canadian Journal of Visual Impairment* 1 (1982): 64–82.

Blunkett, David with Alex MacCormick. *On A Clear Day*. Great Britain: Michael O'Mara Books Ltd., 1995.

Bonner, Keiran. *A Great Place to Raise Kids: Interpretation, Science, and the Urban-Rural Debate*. Montreal: McGill-Queen's University Press, 1997.

Brooks Gardner, Carole. "Passing By: Street Remarks, Address Rights and the Urban Female." *Sociological Inquiry* 50 (1980): 328–356.

Canine Vision Canada. Puppy Manual. Oakville, Ontario: TM.

Chevigny, Hector. *My Eyes Have a Cold Nose*. New Haven: Yale University Press, 1946.

Classen, Constance. *World of Sense: Exploring the Senses in History and Across Cultures*. New York: Routledge, 1993.

Coode, Carole. *Labrador Retrievers Today*. New York: Howell Book House, 1993.

Cooley, Charles Horton. *Social Organization*. New York: Schocken Books, 1909.

Davis, Lennard J., ed. *The Disability Studies Reader*. New York: Routledge, 1997.

Deshen, Shlomo and Hilda Deshen. "On Social Aspects of the Usage of Guide-Dogs and Long Canes." *Sociological Review* 37 (1989): 89–103.

Dickson, Hartwell. *Dogs Against the Darkness: The Story of the Seeing Eye*. New York: Dodd Mead and Company, 1942

Diderot, Denis. "Diderot's Letter on the Blind for the Use of Those Who See." *Reflections: Canadian Journal of Visual Impairment* 1 (1982): 83–122.

Doubt, Keith. *Towards a Sociology of Schizophrenia: Humanistic Reflections*. Toronto: University of Toronto Press, 1996.

Durkheim, Emile. *The Elementary Forms of the Religious Life*. New York: Free Press, 1915.

Eames, Ed and Toni. *A Guide to Guide Dog Schools*, 2d ed. Oakville, Ontario: TM, 1994.

———. 1993 Partners in Independence. *Dog World*, September, 63–76.

Eddy, Jane, Lynette A. Hart, and Ronald P. Boltz. "The Effects of Service Dogs on Social Acknowledgments of People in Wheelchairs." *The Journal of Psychology* 122 (1988): 39–46.

Fogle, B. "Summation: People, Animals, and the Environment." In *Animals and People Sharing the World*, edited by A. Rowan, 177–185. Hanover, N. H.: University Press of New England, 1988.

Foucault, Michel. *Power/Knowledge: Selected Interviews and Other Writings, 1972–1977*. New York: Pantheon Books, 1980.

Gadacz, René R. *Re-Thinking Dis-Ability: New Structures, New Relationships*. Edmonton: The University of Alberta Press, 1994.

Gadamer, Hans Georg. *Truth and Method*. New York: Crossroad Publishing Company, 1988.

———. *The Enigma of Health*. Stanford: Stanford University Press, 1993.

Garfinkel, Harold. *Studies in Ethnomethodology*. Englewood Cliffs, N.J.: Prentice-Hall, 1967.

Goffman, Erving. *The Presentation of Self in Everyday Life*. New York: Doubleday Anchor, 1959.

———. *Behavior in Public Places: Notes on the Social Organization of Gatherings*. New York: Free Press, 1963.

———. *Stigma: Notes on the Management of Spoiled Identity*. Englewood Cliffs, N.J.: Prentice- Hall, Inc., 1963.

Hall, Edward T. *The Hidden Dimension*. New York: Doubleday Anchor, 1966.

Harrison, Felicity and Mary Crow. *Living and Learning with Blind Children: A Guide for Parents and Teachers of Visually Impaired Children*. Toronto: University of Toronto Press, 1993.

Hartwell, Dickson. *Dogs Against Darkness: The Story of the Seeing Eye*. New York: Dodd Mead, 1942.

Hegel, G.W.F. *The Phenomenology of Mind*. Translated by J.B. Baillie. New York: Harper and Row, 1967.

Hickford, Jessie. *Eyes At My Feet*. New York: St. Martin's Press, 1973.

Hill, Melvyn A., ed. *Hannah Arendt: The Recovery of the Public World*. New York: St. Martin's Press, 1979.

Hillyer, Barbara. *Feminism and Disability*. Norman, Oklahoma: University of Oklahoma Press, 1993.

Howes, David, ed. *The Varieties of Sensory Experience: A Source Book in the Anthropology of the Senses*. Toronto: University of Toronto Press, 1991.

Journal of Social Issues: The Role of Animals in Human Society, vol. 49, no. 1 (1993).

Karatheodoris, Stephen. "Blindness, Illusion and the Need for an Image of Sight." *Reflections: Canadian Journal of Visual Impairment* 1 (1982): 31–51.

Knott, Thomas with Dolores Oden Cooper. *The Complete Handbook of Dog Training*. New York: Howell Book House, 1994.

Leder, Drew. *The Absent Body*. Chicago: University of Chicago Press, 1990.

Levin, David Michael. *The Opening of Vision: Nihilism and the Postmodern Situation*. New York: Routledge, Chapman and Hall, 1988.

Macnaughten, Phil and John Urry. "Towards a Sociology of Nature." *Sociology* 29 (1995): 203–220.

Mannheim, Karl. *Essays on Sociology and Social Psychology*. London: Routledge and Kegan Paul, 1953.

Matthews, David Ralph. "Mere Anarchy? Canada's 'Turbot War' as the Moral Regulation of Nature." *The Canadian Journal of Sociology* 21 (1996): 505–522.

Mead, George Herbert. *Mind, Self, and Society from the Standpoint of a Social Behaviorist*. Edited by Charles W. Morris. Chicago: University of Chicago Press, 1934.

Merleau-Ponty, Maurice. *Phenomenology of Perception*. Translated by Colin Smith. London: Routledge and Kegan Paul, 1962.

———. *The Primacy of Perception: And Other Essays on Phenomenological Psychology, the Philosophy of Art, History and Politics*. Evanston, Ill.: Northwestern University Press, 1964.

Michalko, Rod. "Accomplishing a Sighted World." *Reflections: Canadian Journal of Visual Impairment* 1 (1982): 9–30.

———. "The Opening of the Bureaucratic Mind: Putting Good Works into Practice." Paper presented at CIRLA conference, Banff, Alberta, 1995.

———. *The Mystery of the Eye and the Shadow of Blindness*. Toronto: University of Toronto Press, 1998.

Morris, Desmond. *The Human Zoo*. Toronto: Clarke, Irwin and Company, 1969.

Mowat, Farley. *Never Cry Wolf*. Toronto: McClelland and Stewart, 1963.

Neville, Peter. *Dog Behavior Explained: A Self Help Guide*. Great Britain: Carlton Books Ltd., 1991.

Ong, Walter J. "The Shifting Sensorium." In *The Varieties of Sensory Experience*, edited by David Howes. Toronto: University of Toronto Press, 1991.

Pfaffenberger, Clarence. *The New Knowledge of Dog Behavior*. New York: Howell Book House, 1963.

Robson, Howard. "Dog Guide and Blind Person: The Matching Process." *Journal of Visual Impairment and Blindness* 79 (1985): 356–368.

Sack, Harvey. "An Initial Investigation of the Usability of Conversational Data for Doing Sociology." In *Studies in Social Interaction*, edited by David Sudnow. Free Press, 1972.

Said, Edward. "Reflections on Exile." In *Out There: Marginalization and Contemporary Cultures*, edited by John Ferguson, et al, 357–366. New York: The New Museum of Contemporary Art, 1990.

Sanders, Clinton R. "Understanding Dogs: Caretakers' Attributions of Mindedness in Canine Human Relationships." *Journal of Contemporary Ethnography*, 22 (1993): 205–226.

———. "Confronting Species Boundaries: Ambiguity and Trainer's Definitions of Guide Dogs." Paper presented at the Couch/Stone Symposium, July 15, 1996.

Saunders, Blanche. *The Complete Book of Dog Obedience: The Guide for Trainers*. New York: Howell Book House, 1978.

Schutz, Alfred. *Collected Papers I: The Problem of Social Reality*. Edited by Maurice Natanson. The Hague: Martinus Nijhoff, 1973.

Scott, Robert A. *The Making of Blind Men: A Study of Adult Socialization*. New Brunswick, N. J.: Transaction Books, Inc., 1981.

Shapiro, Joseph P. *No Pity: People With Disabilities Forging a New Civil Rights Movement*. New York: Times Books, 1993.

Simmel, Georg. *The Sociology of Georg Simmel*. Edited and translated by Kurt Wolff. New York: Free Press, 1950.

Smith, Dorothy E. *The Everyday World as Problematic: A Feminist Sociology*. Toronto: University of Toronto Press, 1987.

Sudnow, David, ed. "Temporal Parameters of Interpersonal Observation." *Studies in Social Interaction*. New York: Free Press, 1972.

Synnott, Anthony. "Puzzling over the Senses: From Plato to Marx." In *The Varieties of Sensory Experience*, edited by David Howes. Toronto: University of Toronto Press, 1991.

———. *The Body Social: Symbolism, Self and Society.* New York: Routledge, 1993.

Taussig, Michael. *Mimesis and Alterity: A Particular History of the Senses.* New York: Routledge, 1993.

Taylor, Charles. *Sources of the Self: The Making of the Modern Identity.* Cambridge, Mass.: Harvard University Press, 1989.

Titchkosky, Tanya. "The Primacy of Between-ness: A Hermeneutics of Marginality and Art." York University: Ph.D. Dissertation, 1997.

Tucker, Michael. *The Eyes that Lead.* New York: Howell Bookhouse, 1984.

Valentine, Deborah, Mary Kiddoo and Bruce LaFleur. "Psychosocial Implications of Service Dog Ownership for People Who Have Mobility or Hearing Impairments." *Social Work in Health Care* 19 (1993): 109–125.

Van Manen, Max. *The Tone of Teaching.* Ontario: Scholastic-TAB Publications, Ltd., 1986.

———. *Researching Lived Experience: Human Science for an Action Sensitive Pedagogy.* London: Althouse Press, 1990.

Vaughan, Edwin. *The Struggle of Blind People for Self-Determination: The Dependency-Rehabilitation Conflict: Empowerment in the Blindness Community.* Springfield: Charles C. Thomas, 1993.

West, Cornel. "The New Cultural Politics of Difference." In *Out There: Marginalization and Contemporary Cultures,* edited by Russell Ferguson, et al. New York: The New Museum of Contemporary Art and MIT, 1990.

Wieder, D. L. "Behavioristic Operationalism and the Life-World: Chimpanzees and Chimpanzee Researchers in Face-to-Face Interaction." *Sociological Inquiry,* vol. 50 (1980): 75–103.

Wolfe, Alan. *The Human Difference: Animals, Computers and the Necessity of Social Science.* Berkeley: University of California Press, 1993.

Yale, Michael and Jo-Anne Yale. *No Dogs Allowed.* Ontario: Methuen Publications, 1980.

Index